More Praise for *The Confidence Myth*

"*The Confidence Myth* is the handbook for any woman looking to succeed in her career. Helene Lerner cuts through the noise and gets to the heart of what keeps women from succeeding in business—and how to get past it!"

—Barbara Corcoran, real estate mogul and star of ABC's Shark Tank

"Helene Lerner tackles head-on the myths and truths about confidence—a hot topic linked to women's success. Her straightforward, authentic approach incorporates practical tips and exercises to help build your confidence muscle. This book is a treasure trove of advice to help advance your career."

—Sharon Orlopp, Global Chief Diversity Officer and Senior Vice President of Corporate People, Walmart

"*The Confidence Myth* offers practical insights, tips, and tools that can help you move through your fears and spark your confidence. It's an indispensable read for women who want to become empowered and successful while staying true to their values."

—Denise Morrison, President and CEO, Campbell Soup Company

"This is a powerful and heartfelt book about what it actually means to have true confidence. Helene inspires women leaders to tackle the confidence myth and provides actionable advice for women to propel their careers to the next level."

—Sylvia Ann Hewlett, Founding President and CEO, Center for Talent Innovation

"*The Confidence Myth* is a must-read for every professional woman; it provides pragmatic advice for present and future leaders. Helene Lerner's insights are extremely valuable for any woman who wants to develop into a world-class leader."

—Ana Dutra, President and CEO, Executives' Club of Chicago

"Every woman needs to read this book. It confirms you are not alone in your fears and worries while offering solid strategies to get beyond them. I started dog-earing pages I wanted to return to until I realized it would be easier just to dog-ear the ones I didn't."

—Janet Kelly, Senior Vice President Legal, General Counsel and Corporate Secretary, Conoco Phillips

"We all struggle with knowing how to express our own value and move through our fears. This book walks women through these common struggles and helps them emerge as stronger, more confident role models. Helene Lerner's combination of both honesty and insight makes this a valuable tool for women of all ages."

—**Mika Brzezinski, cohost of MSNBC's *Morning Joe***

The
Confidence
Myth

The Confidence Myth

Why women undervalue their skills
and how to get over it

Helene Lerner

BK
Berrett–Koehler Publishers, Inc.
a BK Business book

Berrett-Koehler Publishers, Inc.
1333 Broadway, Suite 1000
Oakland, CA 94612
Tel: (510) 817-2277   Fax: (510) 817-2278   www.bkconnection.com

Ordering Information
Quantity sales. Special discounts are available on quantity purchases by corporations, associations, and others. For details, contact the Special Sales Department at the Berrett-Koehler address above.
Individual sales. Berrett-Koehler publications are available through most bookstores. They can also be ordered directly from Berrett-Koehler: Tel: (800) 929-2929; Fax: (802) 864-7626; www.bkconnection.com
Orders for college textbook/course adoption use. Please contact Berrett-Koehler: Tel: (800) 929-2929; Fax: (802) 864-7626.
Orders by U.S. trade bookstores and wholesalers. Please contact Ingram Publisher Services: Tel: (800) 509-4887; Fax: (800) 838-1149; E-mail: customer.service @ingrampublisherservices.com; or visit www.ingrampublisherservices.com /Ordering for details about electronic ordering.

Library of Congress Cataloging-in-Publication Data
Lerner, Helene, 1946-
The confidence myth: why women undervalue their skills and how to get over it / Helene Lerner.—First edition.
    pages cm
Includes bibliographical references and index.
ISBN 978-1-62656-202-8 (pbk.: alk. paper)
1. Women—Vocational guidance. 2. Women—Psychology. 3. Confidence.
4. Executive ability. 5. Success in business. I. Title.
HF5382.6.L468 2015
650.1082—dc23   2014041877

FIRST EDITION
20 19 18 17 16 15   10 9 8 7 6 5 4 3 2 1

Cover design by Crowfoot/Leslie Waltzer
Book design and production by Beverly Butterfield
Copyediting by PeopleSpeak
Indexing by Rachel Rice

I dedicate this book to the people
who have shared their insights
with me through the years and
the talented women who will
be moved to step up

Contents

Introduction

What would change if you felt more confident? Would you have a better job with more responsibilities, making more money? Would your personal life look different? Would your conversations be more honest? Think about this for a minute.

If you said yes to any of these questions, let's look at some of the reasons why you aren't where you'd like to be. You probably want to address both external and internal factors. Externally, women face cultural prejudices that impede our advancement—we are confronted by gender inequities every day. We get frustrated because sometimes our goals have to take a backseat to navigating through this resistance.

But despite these obstacles, some women have been able to move up to the C-suite. So how did they do it? Do they, internally, have more confidence than the average woman? These questions intrigued me.

As an expert on women's issues, I am often asked how to develop confidence. This question kept coming up, so I thought it was time to write about the important topic of women and confidence. I interviewed a number of successful women leaders to find out their thoughts, and after talking to them and reflecting on my own experiences in the workplace, I realized that Confidence with a capital C is a myth. No one has the confidence issue all sewn up, but there's this pervasive misconception that some of us do.

Confidence is often understood to mean

- Being comfortable with oneself (true)
- Courageously taking action while not knowing the result (true)
- Practicing fearlessness (false)

Fear is actually an inherent part of stepping out in a new way. Too many of us wait until we feel comfortable that *all* of our skills line up before we make a move, and as a result, we miss out on the big breaks needed to advance our careers.

The goal of this book is to demonstrate that most women in positions of leadership who have achieved high levels of success felt shaky at times, but they took action anyway. If they hadn't, they would have missed valuable opportunities to make a difference.

My story

Truth be told, my level of fearlessness varies on any given day, even now. Looking back on my career, I often had to act as if I believed in myself when I was doubtful. My list of achievements—television host, author, diversity consultant, and founder of a popular career women's website—certainly did not come easily to me.

When I started my own business in the mid-'90s, "stressed out" was my natural state of being. My friends thought I was crazy for going out on my own during a recession. Money was of great concern as my husband (at the time) and I had a toddler to support. Despite those circumstances, I knew it was time to leap into action, time to take a smart and calculated risk.

I had a burning desire to empower women and girls by creating a multimedia company focused on the issues of working women. I was very motivated, but I did not know the first thing about producing for television or putting together a website. I had to learn everything from scratch: how to get a distributor, create a sales pitch for potential sponsors, manage a production budget, handle releases and get them executed—the list went on. I definitely did not feel like I had everything under control as I stepped out each day and bumped up against more obstacles.

At first I found it difficult to reach out for support (as a child I was taught to appear self-sufficient), but in time I learned to humble myself and accept help from others. I realized that if I wanted to make big changes, I could not do it on my own. Not everyone was supportive, but more than enough people offered me their time and expertise along the way. One colleague, Suzanne Altfeld, was incredibly generous. She became a mentor to me, offering priceless feedback, celebrating my successes, and motivating me to continue when I made mistakes.

What I know for sure—as a result of my experience and the experiences of other successful women—is that you can have lofty goals and achieve them without feeling like you are in complete command of what you're tackling.

The importance of taking action anyway

Shari Levine, an executive vice president at Bravo Media, told me over lunch that she often interviewed for jobs she would need to grow into. She has used her confidence and straight-talking ability to land several of these positions.

In fact, most senior women leaders have had to take big risks to get bigger jobs. They may have felt shaky and unsure about their qualifications, but they took action anyway. In doing so, they moved closer to their goals. Their commitment to making a difference was greater than any gender prejudice or self-doubt they might have felt.

Reaching a higher level is often an uphill battle, but shying away from the challenge deprives others of our valuable insights. We can no longer wait on the sidelines. My call to action is not just for the leaders at the top but for *all* of us: if you are not making a difference and you know you can, step up. Shari advised jokingly, "Just wear a skirt long enough to cover the fact that your knees are shaking."

I'm sure that men could benefit from some of the material presented in this book. However, I chose to focus on how the traditional concept of confidence relates to women because false perceptions—myths about what confidence is—harm women more than men.

In *The Confidence Code*, journalists Katty Kay and Claire Shipman sift through the research and explore the differences between male and female workers—from the way we process information to the physiology of our brains, to the overt and subtle ways our culture determines who will ascend to high-level positions. They observed that women are seen as underconfident, underestimating their own knowledge and skills. Men, on the other hand, tend to be overconfident,[1] more likely to have an inflated sense of who they are and what they can achieve.

Why shouldn't women step into positions of more responsibility? Why not go for the bigger job, even if you don't have all of the skills required? Why not reject the position you are overqualified for and counter with, "I want the job two levels higher"? Don't listen to the negative voice that whispers, "You don't have what it takes." This attitude stems from prejudice, not truth.

The myth of the highly confident individual without fear must give way to a more realistic assessment of what confidence involves. A confident woman has the whole package: talent, insight, excitement, courage, *and* fear. Confidence is not the absence of discomfort; rather, it is taking action while having conflicting thoughts and sensations. We need to align our definition of confidence with Nelson Mandela's understanding of courage: "I learned that courage was not the absence of fear, but the triumph over it." Real confidence is acknowledging fear and moving forward anyway.

Book overview

My sincere hope for this book is to help women like you redefine confidence (with an acknowledgment that fear and courage are components just as much as talent and insight are) and to persuade you to reach for your next big goal.

I believe that each one of us is called to make an important contribution. This book is a practical tool kit to help you navigate through internal resistance in the service of making your own important contribution. The many qualities we bring to the table, including creativity, connectivity, and a unique perspective, are needed around the globe. Let me support you as you think, dream, and act boldly.

My team at WomenWorking.com conducted an online survey of 535 people, mostly women, covering confidence issues both at work and in our personal lives.[2] Insights and important results from this survey appear throughout the book, along with confidence myths that need to be busted, wisdom from high-level professional women, and Confidence Sparks (exercises, tips, and reflections) to help you move forward in spite of the uneasiness you may feel. A What Would You Do? exercise at the end of each chapter presents challenging scenarios and effective ways of dealing with them. A convenient Power Tools summary helps solidify the main takeaways from each chapter.

The results of the Women and Confidence Survey were clear and consistent, and they confirmed my initial thoughts on this important topic: a perceived lack of confidence holds most of us back, but it doesn't have to. You will never feel 100 percent self-assured as you step out in a bigger way. Moving forward with fear is a skill you develop over time and with practice. And I can tell you from experience that *now* is the best time to test the waters.

Below are short summaries of what you will find in each chapter.

Chapter 1: Transform Fear by Stepping Up

Myth: I can't tackle it now; I'm not ready.
Truth: I can do it. What I don't know I will learn or delegate.

Chapter 1 sets the stage for looking fear in the face as you step out in a new way. Inspiring stories from the women I've interviewed will prepare you for identifying and committing to *stretch goals.*

Chapter 2: Lead with Presence

Myth: It's not possible to learn how to be a dynamic leader.
Truth: Leadership presence can be cultivated and is available to me.

Leading with presence involves presenting yourself authentically, exhibiting poise during stressful times, reading the room, artfully listening, dressing the part, and, especially for women, using power language to assert yourself. Chapter 2 presents skill-building tips in these areas and more.

Chapter 3: Win with Honest Feedback

Myth: When I feel criticized, I react defensively and I can't be objective.

Truth: I have the ability to discriminate, take what fits, and leave the rest.

In order to advance, you must understand how others see you. In our quest for excellence, our perfectionism can get in the way of our ability to accept feedback and grow from it. Chapter 3 provides examples and strategies for processing feedback constructively and determining what's valuable. Useful ways of giving feedback are also offered.

Chapter 4: Create Power Parameters

Myth: If I don't do it, no one else will.

Truth: If I say no, others will pick up the slack, and that will be just fine.

As women, demands on our time come from so many fronts that we can lose sight of our own needs. Our well-being and future success depend on our ability to set limits with people and prioritize what *we* need from day to day. In chapter 4, you will be given strategies for determining your "power parameters" and having the often difficult conversations necessary to create them.

Chapter 5: Stand Out and Attract Sponsors

Myth: The competition for sponsors is fierce—standing out and getting one is too difficult.

Truth: I can attract and build important power alliances.

Awareness has increased in the last several years about the importance of attracting sponsors, people who advocate for you when positions open up. Men have cultivated these powerful relationships for decades, and women can learn a lot from them. You can create these crucial alliances, and chapter 5 will give you the tools to do so.

Chapter 6: Trust Your Inner Compass
Myth: When I am under pressure, I can't tap into my intuitive insight.
Truth: I always have access to my intuition and the ability to use it.
Tough choices are made every day in business, and often we have no precedent to guide our decision making, especially as women travel into uncharted workplace territory. Developing an inner compass can help you navigate the bumps along the way and bust the myths discussed in the previous chapters. Chapter 6 provides tools to help you connect with your inner wisdom and make intuition your professional edge.

Appendix A: Thirty Days of Confidence Sparks
Appendix A includes thirty additional Confidence Sparks. Each will boost your ability to take action and move forward in a positive way toward your next achievement. I encourage you to make reading and reflecting on them a daily practice.

Appendix B: The Women and Confidence Survey
Appendix B includes a discussion and presentation of The Women and Confidence Survey and the methodology used. It also presents the survey questions and results.

Transform Fear by Stepping Up

MYTH

I can't tackle it now; I'm not ready.

TRUTH

I can do it. What I don't know I will learn or delegate.

Our fears can prevent us from achieving great heights of success. They can distort reality and are often grounded in false beliefs, including erroneous messages due to gender prejudice. But when we step up and take action, we move through our fears.

Taking action in itself can bring up fear because we are moving outside our comfort zone. That's okay because being challenged means we are growing. Confidence is the ability to step into uncharted territory and take the next right action, to get comfortable with the uncomfortable.

Giusy Buonfantino, president of North America Baby & Child Care at Kimberly-Clark, faced several challenges when she came to the United States from her native Italy. It was all new territory for her, but she never let fear hold her back.

"I worked with a few men who didn't seem to understand my accent," she confided. "What helped was for me to use hand signals to get my points across. I'd put my hand up at a meeting to express my opinion."[1]

Giusy didn't settle for the status quo, which solidified her position as an innovative thinker and a strong leader. Her advice to women is to keep offering suggestions: "I encourage women to share their unique ideas and not hold back. Voice your point of view. Don't be silent. Get your hand up in meetings," she advises.

David Bidmead, global leader of multinational client service at Marsh, added, "When you leave your ego at the door and stop trying to be the smartest person in the room, your opinions and ideas will be more appropriately valued and appreciated" (and that's applicable to both genders). He told me that to be heard, women should offer insights regularly rather than only expressing the occasional opinion.

I followed that same valuable piece of advice early on in my career at the *New York Times*. I was asked to cover for a senior leader at a top-level meeting, which came as a surprise to me. Those directly above me were out in the field, so I was asked to stand in for them. This was my first significant interaction with top management and a big deal. I hadn't had time to prepare.

The meeting was on the executive floor. As I got off the elevator, I was nervous. But as David suggested, I parked my ego outside the door and walked in the room. I thought to myself, *Just be of service. Offer your help when needed.*

I listened carefully to what was being said. The men in the room were discussing a problem and I had an idea, so I spoke up. Admittedly, my voice was a little shaky, but they listened attentively. As a result of that experience, top management began viewing me as having leadership potential.

↘↙↗↖ **Confidence spark**

**When the voice of fear is saying "hold back,"
see it for what it is. Your fear may be grounded
in a false belief about what will happen if
you put yourself forward. With reflection, you
might find that your fear has been stripped
of its power and that stepping up doesn't seem
as intimidating as before.**

How we limit ourselves

As women, we encounter gender prejudices all the time. Sometimes we may even accept the biases we encounter as true, unaware that we're doing so. For example, many of us have been brought up to play nice. We feel compelled not to rock the boat or appear confrontational, so we refrain from saying or doing what is necessary to get ahead.

But what if instead of trying to be nice, we respond authentically? What would that look like? For one, people would know where we really stand on the issues that are important to us. In addition, we would have more time to focus on making a difference and advancing our careers instead of trying to please other people.

The continually evolving workplace can be stressful and we need vigilance to monitor our thoughts and confront negative self-talk, what I call *mad mind-chatter*, that holds us back. I use this label because to think that we are not capable of achieving greater things is insane. In the Women and Confidence Survey we asked people what they would do to become more confident. Over half (58 percent) responded that they would "counter negative mind-talk with more affirming thoughts." We need to question the old ways of acting that limit us, and we need to adopt new behaviors.

Facebook chief operating officer Sheryl Sandberg says that we hold ourselves back by giving in to self-doubt and "lower[ing] our own expectations of what we can achieve." She urges us to stop "pulling back when we should be leaning in."[2]

Maybe you don't feel like you are ready to "lean in." You still have a lot to learn, and for now, it's better to stay on the sidelines. But no man or woman at any stage of his or her career is ever 100 percent prepared. That is the confidence myth. Now is the time to step up and question that negative belief that counsels you to hold back.

Jill Campbell, now COO of Cox Communications, was almost held back by mad mind-chatter that told her she was not ready to run a Fortune 500 company. When her first chance at the COO role came around, her self-doubt led her boss to think she didn't want the job. Jill's "moment of truth" came when her boss told her he was giving someone else the position.

"When Pat Esser [my boss] suggested that I didn't want the COO position and appointed someone else instead, he could have thrown cold water all over me. I had no idea that I had been projecting self-doubt," Jill shared.

"It worked out fine because the new COO was a huge supporter of mine," she went on. "He helped me get a coach, and I started to handle the issues that stopped me from advancing. I was raised to be 'nice' and not to brag, to play down my abilities. When the COO position opened up again, I knew I could do it. I went to Pat and told him that I wanted to be next."

Not surprisingly, the second time around Jill got the job. She did it by replacing her self-doubt with a more positive and honest appraisal of her abilities. When she believed in herself, she persuaded top management to do so as well.

↘↙
↗↖ **Confidence spark**

**Take inventory of your strengths—actually
make a list of them. Call to mind your current
supervisor and previous managers—what
else would they say about your strengths?
Take this all in.**

When you receive bad news, self-doubt can be the first place you go. In these stressful moments, spot your reactions and use your emotional intelligence to hold on to your sense of power. A few years back, I shared the stage with a senior leader whose company was undergoing a global reorganization. She modeled how to shake off limiting beliefs for over two hundred women attending when she talked about a job she was up for but didn't get.

"I got the news on Thursday that a coworker was promoted instead of me," she revealed. "Of course I was upset, so much so that I took the afternoon off. For a few days, I was on the 'pity pot.' I let myself get angry, sad, and fearful. But then I stepped back from my personal disappointment. I realized he was a better fit for that job than I was. It made sense to move him up," she told us.

By showing her own struggle and explaining how she worked through it, this savvy leader gave the audience valuable insight into how to deal with upsets. She was able to assess the situation objectively and take action accordingly—she decided she needed to take her career in another direction and left the company a few months later.

I too have dealt with career upsets that have been difficult to handle, but by reaching out to my network, I was able to work through them. For example, when a strong supporter of mine unexpectedly did not come on board to fund one of my television shows, I was shocked. She delivered the news compassionately, saying we could revisit sponsorship next year, but I still felt so disappointed—I was barely able to get off the phone without my voice cracking.

I immediately called a friend who listened and supported me to move forward. I made many new business contacts that next year, but I also kept in touch with the sponsor. Sure enough, the following year she was on board again.

Confidence spark

You may not always be able to remove yourself from the situation when you hear bad news. To deal with a disappointment on the spot, take a quick inventory of how you are feeling. Say your boss nixed your proposal without any explanation, and you know it's a winner. He also indicated that he didn't want to talk about it further. Ask yourself: What am I feeling? *Anger. Fear.* Where am I feeling tension in my body? *My jaw is clenched. I have stomach cramps.* What action can I take that is in my best interest? *Do nothing right now.* When you have some distance from the incident, a next step might be to pitch your idea again down the road to your boss or to another manager. Brainstorm with a trusted colleague on how you might go about doing that. After you process the upset, move on.

Do you hold a negative belief that creates self-doubt and keeps you from thinking bigger? Perhaps a parent, teacher, close relative, or boss judged you harshly, and instead of questioning the comment, you believed it. In the Women and Confidence Survey, 54 percent of the respondents who reported that they did not feel confident in the workplace said that "having a leader who micromanages and disrespects me" had inhibited their confidence. Neerja Bhatia, executive coach and founder of Rhythm of Success, advises us to stop identifying with the stressful judgments from our past. If we don't, what has happened will block us from getting what we want.

We must be vigilant and recognize our own mad mind-chatter, turning it around when it rears its ugly head. Regardless of what has happened before, know that you can start to change what's happening now.

How thinking small gets in the way of big breaks

Mad mind-chatter can make us believe that we may not be qualified for a job when we are quite capable of tackling it—this mindset keeps us playing small. Why not aspire to something greater?

I was surprised by the stories of several senior leaders who admitted they didn't want to put themselves in the running for that next powerful position early on in their careers. All too many women seem to feel like they need to have a great number of skills in place to make a move, while men need far fewer skills to say yes. You've probably heard of the internal review at Hewlett-Packard a few years back that showed women within the company applied for open jobs only if they met 100 percent of the criteria listed; men, on the other hand, felt they needed to meet 60 percent of the requirements.[3]

Some women didn't take on higher positions until they received encouragement. Cathy Kinney, former president and co–chief operating officer of the New York Stock Exchange, said it was her boss's belief in her abilities that persuaded her to take a leap. After being in the job for a few months, she questioned why she ever doubted her ability to do it. With smarts and passion, she ran the trading floor of over eight hundred people.

Another woman leader at a major consumer goods company shared this story: "When I had been at the company for two years, a position several levels higher became available, and I was asked to recommend people for the job. It didn't occur to me to put myself in the running. That night, the thought crossed my mind, *Why not* me? I submitted my name the next morning and got the job."

Kathy Waller, chief financial officer of Coca-Cola, advises us to take action despite our fears. She says, "Believe that you will do whatever it takes to be successful, even if you have to take a class or reach out to someone with more experience who can help you get up to speed."

If you aren't feeling sure about stepping up (remember, our take on confidence includes feeling shaky but moving forward anyway), use your nervousness to your advantage. "Nervous energy can help pull the greatness out of you— it makes you overachieve," says Jackie Hernández, COO of Telemundo. And as Debbie Storey, chief diversity officer of AT&T, put it, "My knees have been shaking my whole career."

When considering bigger jobs, let your prospective boss be the judge of whether or not you're right for a position— you owe it to yourself to take a smart risk. "People don't walk into a job with all the tools they need," Jackie reminds us.

Let's bust the myth that "I don't have the skills needed to take that job" and realize the truth: "What I don't know I can learn or delegate." Mobilize the support you need to take a bigger leap—pick one or two people you can call on for expertise and feedback, but also be your own mentor and ask yourself "Why not me?"

⤡⤢ Confidence spark

When interviewing for an ambitious assignment, make a list of the skills you have, the skills you need to learn, and the tasks that can be delegated. Now address your fear of not being able to handle the situation, and see the truth as it is. You have several skills, and you can learn or delegate the rest. Breaking down the job into its various parts may also help. What daily tasks can you do right now? Which ones will you assign to someone else?

Speak up even when wobbly

Undoubtedly you are contributing and making a difference. But are you contributing as much as you can?

Sometimes the most frustrating thing about a job is having the talent and ideas to contribute but feeling like you can't give voice to them. In the Women and Confidence Survey, almost half of all respondents who reported that they didn't feel confident in the workplace attributed their lack of confidence to "feeling disconnected to my job because the work does not leverage my skills."

If you know the answer to a problem and you don't speak up, not only does the group suffer, but you do too. How do you know your solution won't be adopted? We may have a strong and reasonable fear of backlash, but sometimes we can hold ourselves back because of vague misgivings that do more harm than good.

Anne Mulcahy, the former CEO and chairman of Xerox, shared on one of my television shows her personal experience with not speaking up. When she was the chief administrative officer, the CEO at the time, Paul Allaire, was disappointed in her for not voicing her opinions at meetings. He was grooming her to take over the company, and she wasn't talking. Anne did some soul searching and her choices were clear: speak up or step down. She had been with Xerox for many years and knew what the company needed, so she began speaking up. The rest is history: Anne went on to lead Xerox powerfully as CEO.[4]

Years ago, I was at a conference and the presenter wasn't addressing how gender prejudice filters down to all levels of an organization and the difficulty of changing that dynamic. That was the real issue at hand, but I seriously thought of not saying anything because I wasn't sure of the reaction I would get. Yet I knew it had to be addressed. Like Debbie Storey my knees were shaking, but I spoke up anyway. Changing the conversation in the room was more important than playing it safe.

Confidence spark

Set aside some time to write about a work issue that has been bothering you but hasn't been addressed. Get clarity as to what's really going on. Who is involved? Why are you upset? Do you have a concern about speaking up? Does this remind you of a similar situation from your past? Share your observations with a supportive friend and get some feedback. Agree to benchmark with your friend (or someone else) as you take steps toward resolving the problem.

How taking risks leads to big rewards

Too many of us play it safe to feel in control. Somewhere along the way, we started to equate risk with danger instead of opportunity.

In the survey data, respondents' comments indicate a high level of correlation between confidence and the willingness to take risks. Some sample responses were, "[Low confidence] often keeps me from taking risks that less able folks take," and "As I've grown older I have a greater belief in myself, and that has allowed me to be more adventurous in my life."

I have practiced risk taking throughout my career because I believe what I can contribute is important. That isn't to say that I don't feel nervous. I have come to accept that trying something new involves discomfort—and taking risks gets easier with practice. I also have reached out for support. My risk-taking ventures haven't always succeeded, but enough of them did. And even when my efforts did not work out, I learned something valuable from trying.

Ruthie Davis, entrepreneur and shoe designer to the stars, is a consummate risk taker, which has certainly contributed to her success. At UGG Australia, she repositioned the iconic sheepskin boot as "fashion" and started a craze across the United States. After holding several corporate jobs, she launched her own shoe line in 2006. Ruthie attributes her success to "thinking outside of the box, writing my own rules, and being brave."[5]

Rosalind Hudnell, vice president of human resources, global director of communications and external relations at Intel, has taken risks since she was a young woman. She attributes this ability to the support she received from her mother and grandmother. Roz told me, "No matter what risk I took, I knew that if I really fell on my face, the worst possible thing that could happen was I'd go back home—which was a pretty cool place." Roz has tried to pass on her risk-taking confidence to her children by letting them know that she has their backs. Her positive attitude enables her to take risks in her career because, as she describes, if "I don't know anything about this [new project or position], I'm going to have to learn really quickly, and in any way I can."[6]

Why not go ahead and take a leap? Even if your efforts don't work out as planned, the lessons learned will make you wiser. Think like Sandra Dewey, executive vice president and head of business affairs for Turner Entertainment Networks and Cartoon Network Originals. She tells herself, "I'm going to make the best choice I can and if that turns out not to be perfect, I'll keep my eye on it, analyze it, and modify it as I go."

 Confidence spark

> If you're feeling shaky about taking an action that could prove risky, use this exercise to determine if the action is what I call a *best bet*, a smart risk worth taking. First, analyze the pros and cons. Say you're offered a job working for a start-up company. How many pluses and minuses can you list? Which do you have more of? Second, consider the timing and your other priorities. Are you just starting out or have you been in the workforce for a long time? Are you single or married; do you have children? All of these factors go into determining whether taking the risk is worth it. Third and most importantly, listen to your inner voice. What is it advising? If everything

**points to go, then it's time to make a move.
Or maybe you find that the timing is not right.
Don't discard your plans—just put them aside
for now. Reevaluate the opportunity, or
another one just like it, at a later time.**

Letting go of perfection

We need to change the paradigm of what an effective businesswoman is and allow for expertise *and* imperfections to be part of the equation. The women I interviewed admitted to both. When we give up perfectionism, we are better able to step up, speak up, think big, and take risks. Yes, we have had to be twice as good as our male counterparts as a result of our late arrival into the workplace. But no one can keep pace with a standard that can never be achieved.

The pretense of perfection can kill your enthusiasm as well as your ability to move forward. Don't indulge it. Mistakes are part of the growing process. Some of the greatest innovations have come as a result of things going awry. A senior leader once told me that it's okay to make mistakes as long as you don't make the same mistake twice.

Stepping up to a stretch goal

Now is the time to identify a bold goal, one that you feel passionate about. Maybe it's a promotion or taking your career in a new direction. Think big!

Breaking your stretch goal into a series of smaller, doable actions may help. What steps will you need to take to get to your goal? If your goal is a promotion, how can you get more visibility with power players? Which project can you put your hand up for that will showcase your skills and commitment?

What else can you do to show that you are ready to advance? How can you attract a sponsor?

Also, consider the people who can support you as you work toward your goal. Who will give you honest feedback, offer expertise, or just be available to listen as challenges arise? Continue reaching out to these people when needed.

Remember, one action at a time will get you there. Once your goal has been achieved, acknowledge the courage it took and how you have grown throughout the process. Don't stop—find another stretch goal to tackle. Confidence is about stepping up over and over again, looking fear in the face and moving ahead anyway.

What would you do?

Scenario	Hold yourself back	Step up
You are asked to suggest the name of a candidate for a job two levels above you.	You do your research and offer up two names. Yours is *not* one of them.	You offer one name— *yours!*
You are in a meeting with your supervisors and they are talking about a challenge you know how to solve.	You offer no comment. They will probably figure out what you know will work.	You speak up and suggest a solution.
You are visiting a client and he confides in you, explaining that a consultant from another firm dropped the ball.	You listen but do not probe into what he needs because it is not your place.	You ask the client what he needs and offer to get back to him with a plan of action.

Power tools

- **Speak up** when your insights can make a difference. If others make disparaging remarks, the results you bring to the table will ultimately override their negative comments. If the negativity continues, you may need to look for other opportunities.

- **Do a spot-check inventory** throughout the day. Be aware of how you are feeling and thinking. If you are experiencing mad mind-chatter based on unfounded biases, question these thoughts.

- **Find a stretch goal** you are passionate about and consider what you need to do to achieve it. Get a few supporters in place and start taking action, one step at a time.

2

Lead with Presence

MYTH

It's not possible to learn how to be
a dynamic leader.

TRUTH

Leadership presence can be cultivated
and is available to me.

Leading with presence is all about the signals you send
out. It is how you portray yourself—through your words,
actions, and appearance—as someone whom others trust
and want to follow.

Many men and women buy into the myth that the presence exhibited by prominent leaders is something they were
born with. In reality, leading with presence is a skill like any
other; it can be cultivated with awareness and dedicated
practice. Leading with presence involves being authentic,
owning our strengths as well as our weaknesses, and speaking up on issues with integrity and passion.

As you might have imagined, the rules for leading with
presence are much more complicated and nuanced for women
than for men. As women, we face the double-edged sword
of gender stereotypes. The lines between being assertive

or being aggressive, taking charge or being overly ambitious, and being nice or being ineffective are so blurred (by both sexes) that hitting the right note can feel impossible. In *Executive Presence: The Missing Link between Merit and Success*, author and CEO of the Center for Talent Innovation, Sylvia Ann Hewlett, sums up the situation: "If you're tough, you're a bitch and no one wants to work for you, but if you're not tough, you're not perceived as leadership material and you won't be given anyone to work for you. It's a high-wire act that every capable woman has had to perform, and the higher she goes, the more perilous the act."[1]

In this precarious work climate, we women must pick our battles. We need to speak up if we think we can make a difference and it will strengthen our position. But if we think we will be judged poorly for making a point—one that is not high on our agenda—letting someone else pick up the slack might be best. Awareness is key, and we need to apply our best judgment and intuition to each situation.

This chapter offers concrete advice on how to build presence as well as inspiring stories from women leaders who have experienced firsthand the trials and tribulations of being visible and leading the pack. These leaders felt shaky at times, but they continued on. If they had retreated, they would have missed out on opportunities to advance up the career ladder and make a difference. The biggest takeaway from them is that you can act with presence even when you don't feel 100 percent sure of yourself.

Being poised under pressure

In the middle of a challenging time, feeling anxious is normal. Nonetheless, to instill trust and engage others, you must project strength and decisiveness. Of course, you need to be authentic as well, which is where acting like you have everything under control when you don't feel like you do can get tricky. What helps you rise above, says Kim Lubel, CEO of CST Brands, is realizing that you are no different from any other leader. "Everyone is a little uncertain as well," she explained.

During a crisis, women leaders are often tasked with showing empathy as well as demonstrating competence. According to Sylvia Hewlett, "For women in particular, winning more latitude in the public's eye depends on showcasing activities that demonstrate you care about the disenfranchised."[2]

Take Jill Campbell of Cox Communications: A few years ago, she had to consolidate some of Cox's units as the company underwent some changes. "It was hard for our leaders to get through this time," she told me.

Jill led the initiative with the intention of treating everyone with dignity and integrity. She tried to consider how the people who lost their jobs would feel as well as how the "survivors" would respond. The controlled yet empathetic manner in which she handled the layoffs earned her the respect of not only the affected employees but also the department heads under her. Following her lead gave them a compassionate yet effective way to deal with a stressful and difficult situation.

Leadership presence involves humility. As Andrea Zintz, career coach and president of Strategic Leadership Resources, clarifies, humility is not about diminishing your stature but rather involves benevolence, consideration, generosity, and graciousness. By keeping humility in mind, you rise above the challenges to build trust.

Deborah DeHaas, chief inclusion officer for Deloitte, has created "Lessons in Leadership: My Rules to Live By," which help her remain poised under pressure while acting with humility. They were inspired by her mother, who was a strong role model. Deb wrote the rules early in her career as core values to guide her through good and bad times. They help her maintain her composure during the challenges she faces in her leadership roles at Deloitte. The rules were also tested when her previous employer scaled back its operations and later closed its doors in the early 2000s. Deb told me that during this dark time she woke up several mornings at three a.m. wondering what the day would bring. Guided by these core beliefs, she was able to lead with compassion.[3]

Deb generously shares her rules below.

Lessons in Leadership: My Rules to Live By©
- Be true to yourself
- Do the right thing
- Remember that actions speak louder than words
- Put first things first
- Just do it
- Don't forget that there's no *I* in team
- Never underestimate the power of mentors, networks, and sponsors
- Embrace lifelong learning
- Follow the Golden Rule
- Leave a legacy

 Confidence spark

To keep poised in the face of a challenge, give yourself time to explore your reaction to the situation and what choices you have moving forward. If you are not in touch with your feelings about what is happening, you are less likely to act in your best interest or

in the best interests of the others involved. Take a moment to pinpoint your emotions, thoughts, and beliefs about the crisis. Then make a list of strategic actions you can take and the results you think they may yield— including how the people affected might respond.

Reading the room

Leading with presence necessitates self-awareness—the ability to own all of yourself and project your strengths in an authentic way. It is also about being keenly aware of the people around you and how they are feeling.

Understanding the mood of your audience, whether you are talking to a few people in your office or a group of over one hundred in an auditorium, is crucial. To command the room you must first read the room, as Sylvia Hewlett writes, which includes, "sensing the mood, absorbing the cultural cues, and adjusting your language, content, and presentation style accordingly."[4]

Jill Campbell's experiences growing up helped her respect diversity and learn to listen closely, skills she has used throughout her career. Her dad was a psychologist and a professor; his specialty was alcoholism and drug abuse. Her mom was a real estate agent and very independent. Over Christmas and Thanksgiving, lots of different people were in their home, including graduate students and recovering alcoholics. "I learned that you need to spend time with folks and hear their stories to know about them," she told me. Those of us who did not have the exposure Jill had can develop our people skills and emotional intelligence through training and observation.

The most charismatic leaders don't seem to be as concerned with the material they're presenting as they are with getting to know their audiences. Jill, for one, wows her listeners because she's focused on them—what *they* want and need to know. I was at a talk she gave to Women in Cable Telecommunications, and seeing her in action was a pleasure—her authenticity gives her grace and power!

"I'm not going to give the same speech to a group of women in cable, as I would to a group of male executives," Jill explained, adding that time of day enters into it as well. "If it's right before lunch and you see people flipping through your presentation in their meeting materials, you're not going to cover all of it point by point.

"You have to adjust to what they are feeling and what's happening in the room. Are they rolling their eyes? It drives me crazy when a speaker doesn't look at body language and sticks to a canned speech, not aware of what's going on around them."

Kathy Murphy, president of Fidelity Personal Investing, gave this example of how she carefully read the room at a difficult juncture earlier in her career. Her business had just been acquired by ING, a multinational Dutch firm of 150,000 people worldwide. ING's top two hundred leaders were getting together as they do each year, and Kathy was one of only seven women in the leadership group. Not only did she have to deal with being in the minority, she was also learning the international rules of the road. Oh—and she was seven months pregnant.

"One of my guideposts is that it's often a mistake to try too hard too early," Kathy shared. "So I sit back for a time, learn about the culture and what value I can provide, and watch things develop. I think that served me well with Europeans because I'm not perceived as self-promoting or too aggressive (the ugly American). People play into that stereotype because they try to impress too quickly."

Kathy was promoted several times because she was able to read what was important to the board and deliver on it. She realized that ING's board was no different than an American board—the members wanted to see results. And so she focused on producing measurable results.

Speaking with presence

Being able to read the room sets the stage for speaking with presence. Public speaking can be challenging—for many of us it is one of our greatest fears. But the only way to lessen the fear is to get out and speak. And the more you do, the better you'll get.

Your ability to read and command a room can be learned. And the best way to learn is to practice. Kim Lubel is a prime example: "I used to be terrified of speaking in front of a large group. Several years ago at Valero Energy, I was given an assignment that involved the philanthropic side of the business. This project entailed giving speeches to different groups—it was my first exposure to being groomed for leadership. I actually reached out to a coach for help, which made a huge difference.

"I'd write my remarks down—then rewrite them—and would put my notes in front of me when it was time to speak. With practice, I learned that I really didn't have to use them. I try to look at the audience and see how they're reacting, and if I need to redirect my remarks, I do. Nowadays that drives my speech writers crazy."

For Jackie Hernández of Telemundo, envisioning a positive outcome has helped her speak with presence. For her first staff meeting at her former position as publisher of *People en Español*, Jackie envisioned herself passionately speaking to the group. An image of a successful meeting primed her to make it happen.

I am a powerful and passionate keynote speaker, but I wasn't always—I learned by experience and also with the help of a coach, making many mistakes along the way.

Over a decade ago, I delivered a speech at a conference—and I bombed spectacularly. I was speaking at the evening session, right after dinner, and people wanted something light and anecdotal. Instead I gave them a PowerPoint presentation. I totally lost the audience and I felt bad about it. I felt like I had truly let down the person who brought me in to speak.

This experience drove me to get a coach and really hone my speaking skills. I realized how important it was to be authentic, to not show PowerPoint slides when people are expecting something different but instead to tell stories—personal stories, some of which I had told only to my best friends. And if I shared a weakness to get my point across, which I was afraid to do for a very long time, the audience connected with me even more. If someone like me, with my flaws, could be successful, so could they. My story inspired them.

Lee Glickstein, founder of Speaking Circles International, is the transformational speaking coach who worked with me. He underscored the importance of listening to your audience before, during, and after you speak in order to create nonverbal connections. I learned from him that the spark between audience and speaker is ignited as you give the audience your full attention. He also advised me that it's okay to feel your fear but remember that most people want you to succeed.

Nowadays I speak at a lot of events, and I try to find out as much as possible about my audience beforehand. I always get to the venue an hour early so I can greet people as they come into the room. I don't have to connect with everyone verbally, but I can acknowledge them with a glance. My intuition is at play and I trust its guidance. When I am actually on stage, I take a few deep breaths before I begin to speak, and I listen to the sounds in the room—this gets me focused and really present with my audience.

I once spoke with a group of about two hundred women whose company was being reorganized. Thousands of people were going to be laid off. I could feel the tension in the room and the stress these employees were facing. I adjusted my opening remarks accordingly and shared a time when I went through something similar. I acknowledged the discomfort of change and let them know that the decisions I made at the time actually catapulted my career. I shared with them how I took a transitional job, developed new skills, and ultimately left the company to open my own business. They really connected with me.

Confidence spark

If public speaking is a great fear of yours, try practicing first with a few people you are comfortable with, people who you know will be an encouraging audience. Allow for nervousness, but focus on your listeners and their supportive presence. Take a few deep breaths and share something personal that's meaningful for you. Authenticity and vulnerability help create a connection with your audience. A few sessions with a coach might be helpful if you feel the need.

Practicing artful listening

Are you a good listener? When someone is talking, do you really hear what is being said? Or are you just wanting to respond? When someone is withholding, do you make an effort to bring him out? Or are you thinking about your own agenda and filtering his remarks accordingly? I know I'm guilty of not really listening well at times. If I have a personal agenda, it colors the way I hear what people are saying.

A strong leader knows that you don't learn anything if you do all the talking. Jill Campbell's father's favorite saying was, "God gave you one mouth and two ears. There's a reason for that." Executive coach Alan Allard told me, "Listening shows respect, even if you don't agree with what the person is saying."

Listening is an area where the gender stereotype works in our favor. According to Jill, "Women are so much better at listening. I see it in the boardroom; men just keep talking over each other—they enjoy hearing themselves speak."

Sandra Dewey of Turner Entertainment and Cartoon Network is very serious about the key role listening has played in her success. "It didn't come about because I am so brilliant. If I didn't listen to people and take their expertise seriously, I would not have been able to make the best decisions."

To communicate effectively and make the best decisions, you need to know what people are thinking about. Make it a practice to ask them. When Kim Lubel became CEO of CST Brands, she did roundtable after roundtable with her employees, taking copious notes about what they thought was needed. "I reread and organized them into issues to pursue. Now we're executing some of those items."

Artful listening goes beyond hearing the words a person is saying. It is about picking up on other cues, such as tone of voice and demeanor. In addition, it's about tuning in to who is not speaking and what is not being said.

Debbie Storey of AT&T makes it a point to solicit comments from those who are not forthcoming. She told me, "It's not always the vocal people at the table you need to worry about. In many cases, it's the people who aren't saying anything—or are being uncharacteristically silent. You need to hear from the quiet dissenters as well.

"It's easy for the better choice to be overlooked by letting the vocal folks lead the way and not hear from people who sit back. You have to get them talking to bring out every perspective. That's how you get a better solution. And you've gotten them on board when the time comes to move forward."

Similarly, Kathy Waller of Coca-Cola makes it her responsibility to decipher what her team members are not saying. Artful listening is important to her leadership: "I have a great team and they work really hard, putting in lots of hours, particularly during quarter closes, year-end closes, and special projects. I have to pay attention to the toll it takes on them. I guarantee you, if I go and say, 'How are you doing?' they will say, 'Fine.' I know better. I know when they are not fine."

⌄⌄ ⌃⌃ Confidence spark

One of the best ways to listen to someone is to tune in to the sound of his voice. He may be saying one thing but meaning something else. Focus on the quality of his tone—does he sound stressed or confident? What do you know about him that can help you figure out what he is really saying? If thoughts come up that distract you, just keep focusing on his voice to heighten your awareness of his real motivation and mental state.

A colleague shared a story with me about how she took artful listening a step further. By focusing on her two managers' distinct styles and language when they spoke to her, she learned how to communicate more effectively with each of them.

Originally she had been dealing with a manager whose style was straightforward. He liked information delivered succinctly and appreciated bottom-line results, so that's what she gave him. When he moved on to a different job, a new manager came in who had a totally different style.

At first she spoke in the same way to the new manager, but she quickly realized that he wasn't responding well. She observed his interactions with other people and noticed that he enjoyed hearing stories. She also paid close attention to his language and the words and phrases he often used. The next time she presented to him she started with an anecdote and incorporated some of his lingo into her pitch. This immediately caught his attention and got his buy-in.

⟍⟍ Confidence spark

Try this with someone you don't know well who is in a position of authority: The next time you have a meeting with her, pay close attention to how she expresses herself.

How does she start the meeting—does she get right into it or does she prefer sharing personal information first? Does she seem relaxed or formal? What words and expressions does she commonly use? When you need to get an important point across, try using the same language and a similar style of speaking and notice how she responds.

Be attentive to the words, style, and expressions that people are using. Use common language to build a bridge with a person to establish greater rapport and understanding. Being a strong leader means inspiring those around you. A person who identifies with the language used is more likely to identify with your message. You may already be familiar with a training program that explores the differences in communication styles (there are quite a few), but if not, you may want to check one out.

Dressing the part

Being at the helm means you are *always* on stage, and that means you *always* have to look the part of a leader. This is especially true for women. "You may think you're like everybody else, but you're not. Women are held to a higher standard about how they look," Jill Campbell warned.

A woman Jill coached was showing up for work dressed like the Woody Allen character Annie Hall—very bohemian. Because of her appearance, she was being discounted by her colleagues and superiors. When Jill pointed out what was happening to her, this woman began to dress differently. Sure enough, both men and women changed their perspectives about her ability to lead.

Research from the Center for Talent Innovation backs up Jill's story. Reflecting on the data, Sylvia Hewlett remarks, "Our survey respondents generated a list of appearance blunders for women that's literally twice as long as the list they generated for men. It would appear that women are judged, and found wanting, on many more visual attributes than men. . . . In addition to the length of the list, women tend to be judged more harshly than men."[5]

Charisse Lillie, vice president of community investment of Comcast Corporation and president of the Comcast Foundation, recommends dressing up rather than dressing down. For her, it's about conveying the image of where you want to be, not where you are. "At Comcast, if you're a leader with credibility, you're not going to come to work in khakis or jeans," Charisse explains.

At the same time, Debbie Storey thinks it's important not to subjugate your individuality: "I always dressed professionally, but it didn't stop me from being a little quirky and on the edge."

Navigating the territory can be tricky, but dressing the part can also give you a boost—that's what Kathy Waller found during an important meeting. When she was promoted to chief of internal audit, Kathy was invited to a meeting with the top 150 leaders at the company. Not only was this the first time she participated in this meeting, it was her first meeting with company leaders and the new chairman.

"I always try to avoid overthinking things and focus on being authentic. But this meeting was special, and I wanted to get it right. So, as I normally do, I talked with my sister Audrey about it. Obviously she couldn't tell me what to expect at the meeting—I sought the advice of others for that—but her suggestion was great: 'Figure out how to feel good about yourself while you're there, and make sure what you wear is appropriate to the setting.' In preparation, everything I owned was pretty much on my bed. My color is red, so I wore red."

Wearing red gives Kathy a lift, so she wears the color whenever she needs to sharpen her game. It gives her a confidence boost.

 **Confidence spark**

Think of yourself in a job two levels higher than the one you have now. Imagine what you'd be doing. What do you look like— how are you dressed? Do you seem poised and in command? Reflect on some of the women leaders who are actually at that level now. How do they carry themselves? How do they dress? In preparing for what you will wear to work tomorrow, keep these images in mind. Pick your clothes accordingly. Also, practice carrying yourself as a leader— shoulders relaxed and back with your head held high as you walk.

What would you do?

Challenge	Hold yourself back	Lead with presence
You need to share some bad news with your team.	You tell them what's going on in a low tone and make little eye contact.	You are direct and to the point. Your tone is firm but empathetic and you occasionally offer a smile.
A conflict between people you supervise has come to your attention. It's been going on for days.	These are two adults. Letting them deal with it themselves is better than your getting caught in the crossfire.	You get both parties together and hear both sides. You acknowledge where each is coming from and find a compromise.
You have been asked to step in for your boss, who is out ill, and give a speech to shareholders this evening. You have never done anything like that before.	You doubt that you will be able to do a good job because you're not a public speaker. You try to get someone to cover for you.	You get on the phone and set up a coaching session. You go over the speech a few times with your coach. You feel a bit nervous but know you can deliver.

Power tools

- **Be people sensitive.** Know your audience (whether one or many) and understand how you need to communicate in order to bring about change.

- **Learn to artfully listen.** Go beyond the words people are saying to know what they are really feeling.

- **Observe powerful women** and note the way they dress. What makes them look like leaders? Can you see yourself dressing in a similar way? If not, how would you dress differently?

- **Become more self-aware.** When you have to handle a stressful situation, own how you feel before you take action. When you are being authentic, you'll more easily be able to maintain your poise.

Win with Honest Feedback

MYTH

When I feel criticized, I react defensively
and I can't be objective.

TRUTH

I have the ability to discriminate, take what fits,
and leave the rest.

Many people don't like confrontation, so telling you
what you are doing right is easier for them than saying what
you're doing wrong. But if no one speaks honestly to you,
how will you know what is getting in the way of your moving up?

Feedback tells us how we are really being perceived, so if
we are not getting it, we need to ask for it. Although feedback may not be easy to seek out or hear, once we get it
we can take what fits, make the necessary adjustments, and
discard what doesn't. In my interviews with women leaders, they all agreed that honest feedback is a must. What we
don't know will hurt us.

Jill Campbell, COO of Cox Communications, almost derailed her career because she didn't realize the effect she was having on people. Thankfully she received some constructive criticism and was able to put it to use.

"Before I was COO, I was having some problems because I was very emotional. I'd get pissed off about things in front of groups and that would scare people. I had been with the company for thirty years, so I thought it was okay. But it wasn't. My [career] coach told me, 'They're scared of you, and that's killing you.' When I heard it said that way, I thought, *Wow, this is important. I need to change.*

"In cable, people cuss a lot. I have really toned that down. It wasn't hard to do, which surprised me. If it was going to block me in my career, I knew I needed to fix it. I would have never done that if I didn't get that feedback."

I have gotten similar feedback about how people read me when I am stressed and under a deadline or when an unexpected setback happens: I tense up and my voice gets firm. My staff reads this behavior as if they have done something wrong, even when they haven't. That's not how I want them to feel.

It was suggested to me that during those times I raise my voice instead of lowering it and keep my tone as neutral as possible. I don't always succeed at doing this, but I do try. I believe my staff is as grateful for the feedback I received as I am!

Lisa Kudlacz, general manager of global interventional pain management at Halyard Health, shared how the honesty of a colleague helped her develop her public speaking skills:

"Early in my career I made a major presentation to the executive team, and I was quite nervous. I knew it didn't go as smoothly as I would have liked. After people left the room, a coworker approached me and asked if I would like some feedback. I nodded. He mentioned that I had used the word *um* seventy-five times. I was unaware and practiced not doing that with my subsequent talks, making sure not to utter that word!"

Take the stigma out of feedback

Why do we take feedback personally? I believe the issue goes back to perfectionism, which I discussed in chapter 1. There is a stigma attached to being anything less than perfect, and we feel exposed when we find out through critiques that we aren't.

Confidence is about showing up and moving forward as we are, not having it all together and never making mistakes. When we allow for mistakes, we are growing. The question then becomes, how do we deal with the discomfort of hearing constructive feedback so we can process it and move forward?

Time can take the sting out of criticism. One method recommended by a survey respondent is to "write about a misunderstood action, [and then] try to analyze it some days later." Another suggested, "Continue to reflect on a track record [of good work]; know that mistakes are learning opportunities."

Early in my career, I would react too quickly to unexpected feedback, and on several occasions I said things I later regretted. Here's an example of how I could have sabotaged myself, but chose not to.

In 2000 I created the website WomenWorking.com as a companion to the television shows I hosted and produced about career women. Before the site was launched, I sent an e-mail to colleagues and friends asking them to preview the site. My team was exhausted—we had spent several intense days working to meet our deadline, and I really didn't want to hear feedback that would require reworking the site. I wanted people to tell me the site was great and offer to refer their networks to it.

Most people gave great comments and offered to publicize the site. I was given very few suggestions. However, Ellen Griffith, a colleague of mine, listed multiple items that needed addressing. I got her response in the early evening when I was tired and hadn't had dinner yet. I was about to send her a less than gracious e-mail defending each point (without really addressing her concerns), but I didn't. Thank God! Instead, I went home, had dinner, and slept on it. In the morning I read the e-mail again and Ellen was right—I saw several things we needed to fix. I wrote back and thanked her for her feedback, and my staff made the appropriate changes. Fifteen years later our website is very successful, and Ellen is part of my inner circle, as I am of hers.

The moral of the story: don't react, especially when you are hungry and tired! Process the feedback at a time when you can take an honest look at what is being said.

When you are face-to-face with someone and you get an unexpected critique, handling the feedback can be difficult. I have learned to pause and repeat what is being said—this gives me distance from the remark. I acknowledge the person, let her know I need time to digest it, and tell her I'll get back to her shortly. I then assess what I've heard to determine what is true about it and what isn't. If I feel the need, I talk it out with a trusted friend.

Here is the method Andrea Zintz, career coach and president of Strategic Leadership Resources, uses to deal with harsh advice: "When I receive feedback that is hard to hear,

I retreat a little to manage my reaction. Taking a breath is the first step, and then I turn inward and ask myself: 'Should I take this personally? How can I see this from the other person's point of view?' This calms me down. I can then go back and thank that person from a centered place and process what's useful."

No matter how high up on the totem pole you are, feedback can be difficult to take. Kim Lubel of CST Brands still finds it a challenge. "When I disappoint someone—that's hard for me. I can probably count on one hand the number of times that has happened. But when it does, I try to understand why I did what I did and figure out what to do next," she confided.

One of the people that Kim can count on for honest feedback is Bill Klesse, former CEO of Valero Energy, where Kim used to work. "Bill is judicious with his remarks. When he speaks, it is important to listen," she said. And now that Kim is at the helm of CST Brands, she checks in with the store employees to hear what's on their minds. "If I don't ask for their candid observations, I'm not going to get them."

Kathy Murphy of Fidelity Personal Investing also touches base with her staff on a regular basis. In addition to giving candid critiques, she asks her direct reports for feedback about herself. Kathy keeps a list of their comments, looking at them periodically to ensure she continues to improve her skills.

When unsolicited, criticism from your team can be the hardest to take—but it can also be the most valuable. Look at how Kathy Waller of Coca-Cola, moved through her defensiveness to really hear what her team needed: "I was talking with my team about a problem we were having. Afterward, one of my direct reports remarked that I didn't smile once during the meeting. I felt myself getting defensive—it wasn't a funny situation. But I didn't react. Later I realized that they needed a sign that we would get through this challenge. I believe now that having a positive outlook when times are challenging is the responsibility of a leader."

⤢ Confidence spark

Try this the next time you receive feedback and find yourself getting defensive. Take a few deep breaths and repeat back what has been said to show that you have understood. Doing this will give you a little distance from reacting in a way you might regret. Later on you can reflect on what fits and what doesn't. If you need support, get input from a trusted colleague.

Debbie Storey of AT&T developed a thick skin through the years by seeing feedback as a way of expanding her skill set, and also by cultivating a group of trusted advisors that she could bounce the critique off of.

"I remember how devastated I was early on when I was told I was too competitive—I thought someone didn't like me," she shared. Her career coach suggested that she talk to other people to get their perceptions. In doing so, she was able to gain some perspective.

"Feedback is not personal; it's just business," Debbie advises. If she needs to, she consults with people she respects. "I sit down and ask them what they think. Do they see it that way? Should I work on it or let it go?"

Debbie also encourages her supervisors to talk candidly about areas she needs to develop. She asks for feedback directly if it is not being given. She tells them, "It's nice to know that there are good things that I'm doing, but that doesn't help me improve. Please share with me something that will give me an opportunity to grow."

Think about feedback as your opportunity to grow. Knowing the behaviors that are holding you back from advancing is the first step to making the necessary adjustments. As Facebook COO Sheryl Sandberg puts it, "The upside of painful knowledge is so much greater than the downside of blissful ignorance." She suggests soliciting feedback from colleagues by asking them the following questions: "How can I do better?" "What am I doing that I don't know?" "What am I *not* doing that I don't see?"[1]

 Confidence spark

> **A disconnect may exist between how you are perceived and how you think you come across. To gain perspective, ask a colleague what she sees. For example, ask, "With my team, do I come across as passionate and caring?" Listen to what she says, and pause before responding. Be open to asking another question if appropriate.**

Take in what's useful; discard what isn't

In the end, you are the one who has the final say on what you need to work on and what you should ignore. But determining which is which can become more difficult if you're in an environment where you don't trust the people giving you feedback or when the feedback is presented in an unhelpful way.

When you are unclear of the motivation of a person, Charisse Lillie of Comcast advises that you fall back on your intuition: "Maybe you decide, 'I'm going to take this with a grain of salt.' But ask yourself too, 'Is there a nugget of truth here—is there something that I have to work on?' I ask myself that even if I know the person does not have the best intentions in offering advice."

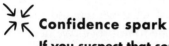 **Confidence spark**

If you suspect that someone is not sincere with the feedback he gives, trust your gut—you are probably right. The best way to deal with him is to be professional. Don't argue or engage; make a note of anything that rings true, and move on.

Why is it hard to give feedback?

We know that receiving feedback is difficult, but giving it can be just as awkward. A number of reasons exist why people are nervous about offering feedback, especially to women. The litigious environment in this country and the threat of being accused of discrimination or harassment is a major reason. Charisse Lillie gives an example from her own experience: "I'm a labor and employment lawyer. I've observed in my practice that some supervisors were afraid to speak with their supervisees candidly. They got nervous, particularly since they were afraid of being accused of sexism or racism by a 'diverse' employee. But they were not doing anybody a favor by holding back and not giving clear and honest feedback."

I have heard that some male managers have a difficult time giving feedback to women because they think we will break down and cry. That's unfortunate because managers who withhold feedback are doing both themselves and their employees a major disservice. Help them (and yourself) by being open to honest feedback and inviting it when it is not given.

Offering negative feedback can be difficult for both sexes. For women in particular, the notion of playing nice can get in the way of being truthful about what we see and saying what needs to be done for someone to improve. We need to get over this mindset and learn how to provide honest feedback concretely and directly.

Sandra Dewey of Turner Entertainment and Cartoon Network learned the value of being direct during serious conversations when she first started managing people: "I made the classic rookie error—the harder the conversation, the more I tried to soft pedal it. When I had to fire someone, I would start off by saying, 'You know, you're great at many things, and, by the way, you're terrible at others, so I'm letting you go.' People walked out very confused. They were wondering, 'What just happened?'

"What I came to realize is it's more of a gift to say it directly. My mantra is 'direct and kind.' So if I have to fire someone, I'll say, 'As much as it pains me to tell you this, you're not right for this job, and we've reached that conclusion. I know you will do well at other things. If you want me to be more specific about why we feel this way, I can.'"

Kathy Murphy believes that candor is a sign of respect. If her group is circling around an uncomfortable issue, not being direct and honest, she will insist they be candid with each other and get the issues on the table: "If there's a concern about an employee, and that individual doesn't know what he is doing wrong, it won't be possible for him to work on that behavior and potentially progress in his career," she shared.

Kathy thinks skirting the issue is just as bad as not giving feedback at all. "You don't want to create an environment where people think they can only give good news or say, 'We are all doing great,' and behind the scenes negative information is disclosed."

Jill Campbell distinguishes between feedback that might lead to an employee exiting the company or being let go, and feedback on behavior that needs to be tweaked. In the first case, which has more serious consequences, she explains, "People tend to get defensive, or they don't believe you. That's when you need to be much more direct."

Kathy Waller believes that more managers need to be candid. If they aren't, employees will continue to act in ways that could derail their careers. She gives an example of being direct and to the point with an associate whose job was on the line: "It was a very difficult conversation. I needed to get this person's attention and I did. I said, 'Look, we need to talk about your future here and whether you have a future here.'"

While it's especially important in serious encounters, being direct is a good tactic for lower-stakes, day-to-day interactions as well. Giving a concise example of how someone can improve his performance is also helpful. But most importantly, don't let problems pile up. A laundry list of what someone is doing wrong is enough to put any person in a closed, unreceptive state.

Table 1 on the next page offers some pointers to help you deliver honest feedback in a direct way.

Table 1. Honest Feedback Pointers

Situation	Feedback
An employee is in the position of losing his job.	Don't downplay the situation. Be candid with him.
An employee is a high potential candidate.	Give concrete advice, emphasizing that she is being groomed for management, and this is part of the strategy for getting her there.
An employee is just starting out her career.	Use examples. Role-play if the situation calls for it.

One last point to keep in mind is that not all situations can be improved, no matter how well-founded your comments are. Sometimes women may experience backlash from those unwilling to hear or accept their suggestions or managers who don't agree with their take on the issue. While you should make a point of giving (and asking for) feedback, trust your intuition to determine whether a situation warrants putting yourself in a precarious position.

 Confidence spark

When giving feedback, be calm, clear, and direct. If you're trying to help someone improve, be specific about what he could do better and give an example. Use positive language—for example, say "Try doing this . . ." not, "Stop doing that . . ." Be compassionate. Think about how he will likely feel.

What would you do?

Scenario	Hold yourself back	Win with honest feedback
You receive some unexpected feedback from your boss. He is disappointed in the way you handled an account.	You are surprised and start to get defensive. He gets more annoyed by your reaction.	You can feel yourself getting defensive, but you pause before you say something you will regret.
Someone you supervise is coming in late and leaving early on a regular basis. You know you need to talk with her and the conversation will be difficult.	You talk around the issue. You aren't clear about what the point is.	You are direct and speak concisely. You've role-played the situation with a friend to make sure you are prepared for your staff member's reaction.
You overhear your manager talking about a situation you handled poorly. You have not discussed the incident with him yet.	You avoid bringing the situation up and hope he does as well. You know what went wrong, and you're feeling bad about it.	You address the situation as soon as you can with him, getting his take on how it could have been handled better. You thank him for his candor.

Power tools

- **Practice detachment.** Don't take feedback personally. It's how we find out what's in the way of our advancement.

- **Use your intuition** to distinguish which advice is useful and which is not. If you need help telling the difference, reach out to a trusted colleague.

- **Be direct** and determine what is important to address when giving feedback. Use an example to illustrate your point.

Create Power Parameters

MYTH

If I don't do it, no one else will.

TRUTH

If I say no, others will pick up the slack,
and that will be just fine.

In January 2014 I was a guest expert on CNN International's *World One* with former host Zain Verjee. We were joking around and I asked her what she thought the most important two-letter word for women was. Zain came up with a great answer: *Me!* But that wasn't what I had in mind. The two-letter word I was thinking of was *No.*[1]

Let's face it. We are all spread too thin. With our jobs, social obligations, home lives, child care, elder care, and community responsibilities—whatever your personal combination is—most of the time we are stretched, perhaps to the limit.

We diminish our power when we are in such a state. That is why creating power parameters—defining your boundaries, choosing your commitments, saying no when necessary, and protecting your time—is so important. Yet many of us struggle with asserting ourselves in this way.

When we set boundaries, we may feel shaky because we are not sure what someone's reaction will be. But the payback is that we are being true to ourselves, knowing our limits, and prioritizing what we need. When we act in this way, we gain confidence. In fact, can we really feel confident if we are not authentic? I don't think so.

In the Women and Confidence Survey, 42 percent of question respondents said they would "say no to things without feeling guilty" if they felt more confident. This chapter offers advice on how to negotiate power parameters with others and yourself and how to minimize guilt when making smart choices that benefit you but have consequences for those around you. We will explore saying no to what does not serve you, getting others to respect your boundaries, and the importance of making time for you.

Why is it so hard to say no?

Why do we say yes when we mean no? Is it because we are people-pleasers? As I've mentioned in previous chapters, many of us are taught as children to play nice and avoid making waves. I certainly was. For this reason, we may feel like we don't have permission to say no.

Some of us find it hard to say no because we are afraid that friends or colleagues will think poorly of us if we turn them down. I have wasted a lot of time in my life trying to assess what people would think if I said no to them. I've failed to realize that I can't control what anyone thinks whether I say yes or no, so it's better to be authentic from the start.

In my early twenties I was taking part in a workshop that went toward my master's in education. The leader was making the point that we need to set our boundaries. He rattled off several requests of me, one after the other, and I had to respond yes or no. I found this tough to do because I was not used to thinking about what I wanted, just what was best for everyone else. I needed some inner work and help from a professional to develop my voice and become comfortable with risking the displeasure of others if I said no. Now, my goal is to support other women in getting to that place as well.

People pleasing takes a heavy toll on us. If I am feeling stretched and I say yes when I really mean no, I either end up resenting the person who asked for my help or I resent myself because I should have declined. Being genuine is better than being nice and that includes saying no.

People pleasing can be particularly harmful for women in the workplace. In an article for *The Nation*, writer Jessica Valenti put it this way, "Women adjust their behavior to be likable and as a result have less power in the world."[2]

For Facebook COO Sheryl Sandberg, wanting to be liked was one of the first things she had to let go of to be successful at her job. In *Lean In for Graduates*, Sheryl relates the story of her first formal review with CEO Mark Zuckerberg. She writes, "He said that when you want to change things, you can't please everyone."[3]

Jackie Hernández of Telemundo also warns of the pitfalls of being too agreeable. "It doesn't get you where you need to be," she explains. "If a man people pleases, it's a different thing. When we do it, we look weak, not tough enough, because we just want people to be happy. The minute you find yourself just saying yes, you have to ask yourself *why?*"

If you find yourself about to say yes against your better judgment, don't give in. Take a moment before you answer to remind yourself that your priorities are more important than acquiescing. As with digesting feedback, taking time before reacting can lead you to a different behavior.

A helpful tactic for saying no is being respectful but honest. If your coworker asks for help on something you know she can figure out for herself and you have your own time-sensitive projects to deal with, try saying something like "I'm on a deadline, and I can't help you now. But what you're doing is similar to how you handled the XYZ project. Use the same strategy." This approach has the great advantage of letting someone down gently and also being truthful.

Here is another example of how one woman learned to say no with the help of a friend. This smart but too-agreeable woman was spread too thin and the stress started to take a toll on her health. Her friend insisted that she tell anyone requesting her time that she would have to check with her "scheduler" (in reality, her friend) before taking on a new project. If the request was not worth her time, she came back to the requester with, "I'm sorry; my scheduler has advised me there's no room for anything new for the next several months."

Sometimes we find it difficult to know when it's in our best interest to say no. We know setting boundaries is important, but the line can be blurry. Here are some examples culled from my experience and that of other women on when saying yes is appropriate and when it is best to say no. You could probably write your own list as well.

Say yes when
- It is an emergency and no one else is left at work to help out.
- Taking the assignment will give you heightened visibility with top management.
- You've said no several times recently, and you don't want to lose an office ally.
- What's being asked doesn't require much of your time.

Say no when

- You are overworked and one more commitment will totally overwhelm you.
- You've moved on to another job and a coworker from your former assignment is constantly asking for advice in the form of evening e-mails.
- You're not that fond of the person asking for help, and you don't want to go out of your way for him.
- You've been working late every night for a week and a half, and your family needs some quality time with you.

If it is unclear whether to say yes or no, write out the pluses and minuses of saying yes. Whichever column has more is the way to go.

Setting boundaries with yourself

Another reason why women don't say no enough is that we feel we should be able to do it all. By letting go of a do-it-all, have-it-all mentality, we give ourselves room to be better at what we *can* do and enjoy more of what we *do* have.

When we hold ourselves up to unachievable standards of productivity and excellence in our work and personal lives and something slips through the cracks, it can be hard to accept. In the Women and Confidence Survey, more than half of respondents who reported not feeling confident in their personal lives said that a major confidence detractor was not living up to their expectations of themselves. If impossibly high personal expectations and perfectionist behavior are undermining your confidence, maybe it's time to be more realistic about what you should expect from yourself.

Kathy Waller of Coca-Cola is like so many women I know (including myself) who has had to work on letting go of unrealistic personal standards. "It's not people that are the problem—it's *me* putting pressure on myself. It's easier to make better choices when I realize that," Kathy shared. "I have gotten much better at recognizing when I need a time-out. I say to myself, 'I'm going to have an overreaction unless I back off.'"

You may feel like you should be doing more, and you will encounter people who ask you to do unreasonable things in time frames that are impossible to meet. With awareness and the desire to assert what you need for your well-being, you can set limits so you don't crash and burn. In the next few sections, we will explore how to do just that.

Make your no someone else's yes

Charisse Lillie of Comcast used to feel like she had to do it all—she compared her overachieving tendencies at work to planning a dinner party for thirty-five people and taking on all the cooking, serving, entertaining, and most of the cleaning herself. Now she does the cooking but also involves others as part of the mix. On the nonprofit front she brags, "I call myself a great nominator because saying no gives me an opportunity to bring other people to the table. My no is somebody else's yes."

Instead of saying yes to one more responsibility that will take you over the top, think about how you can find an alternative that will be a win for everyone. Here's an example:

Charisse received an honorary degree from a local college, and she was later asked to join its board. Doing so, however, wasn't the right fit for her at the time. Instead of just saying no, she declined politely and then offered up the name of a woman whom she thought would be a terrific candidate. The result: "My colleague is happy, the president of the college is happy, and I'm happy," exclaimed Charisse. She made her no a yes for all parties involved.

Negotiating power parameters

If you've made a habit of saying yes a lot, you may find it hard to break the cycle. That's where power parameters come into play. Being clear to yourself and others about where you stand and what your priorities are can help you speak up even when you're wary of saying no. Negotiating your power parameters is a way of asserting yourself and establishing your direction and goals.

How career women negotiate their promotions, salaries, benefits, et cetera is a widely studied area. The research shows that negotiating can be a difficult process for women because the consequences of standing up for ourselves can be much harsher than for men.[4] Facebook's Sheryl Sandberg calls it "trying to cross a minefield backward in high heels."[5]

Research suggests that women may not put themselves out there because both men and women hold female employees to a different standard. It makes sense not to piss off the boss. On the other hand, if you don't ask, you don't get.

These inequities are probably not going to change anytime soon, but we can still step up and negotiate powerfully for what we need now. The women interviewed for this book maneuvered around the unique difficulties women face as they advanced. Here are some of their strategies.

The first step in negotiating your power parameters is figuring out what is most important to you. Debbie Storey of AT&T, offered up a great metaphor for how to determine your personal and professional boundaries: "It's a matter of assessing what you're juggling at the time," she explained. "With all the balls you have in the air, which ones are rubber—if you drop them, they will bounce for a while—and which ones are crystal—if they drop, you'll never get them back. Those you need to set boundaries around."

Early on in her career, Debbie learned to assert herself when the issue was important: "I was a single mom and my son was four years old. At work, I was the only one around the table who was female. The meetings would run over and I was the one sweating, concerned that my son wouldn't be picked up in time from school.

"I went to my boss and asked for his help. I let him know I would work overtime as much as needed, but I had to know the days in advance so I could make the necessary arrangements. I also negotiated that I would not be the first person called when emergencies came up on weekends."

Once you have determined which balls you're juggling are rubber and which are crystal, think about what you can do to make the situation a win-win, like Debbie did. She needed to negotiate a power parameter around her family commitments, but that didn't mean she was taking a backseat at work. To make sure her boss saw that, she offered concrete examples of how she could continue to step up at the office, such as working overtime when it could be planned in advance.

Shying away from uncomfortable negotiations that involve taking a stand and setting limits is natural. Lessen the anxiety by figuring out how to make what *you* want attractive to the other party. The most important step is careful forethought and framing.

For example, when negotiating for a raise, Sheryl Sandberg advises framing the discussion in terms of the common good. She recommends positioning yourself as connected to the company at large, by using *we* instead of *I*. "A woman's request will be better received if she asserts, 'We had a great year,' as opposed to 'I had a great year,'" she writes. With a simple pronoun change, your negotiation is reframed as what is best for the organization.[6]

The last point I want to cover about negotiation is allowing yourself to think bigger. That's where confidence comes in. Ask for more than what you want, even if you think you won't get it. Be bold. If you aim high, you are much more likely to end higher and be better off than you were at the start.

Confidence spark

You may know this already, but it's a good reminder. The rule of negotiating is to find a way that both parties win. Beforehand, figure out where you will be flexible (the rubber balls) and what is nonnegotiable (the ones made of crystal). Let the person know at the beginning of your meeting that you are interested in creating a win-win situation for both of you. Do your homework. What does he need from you? How can you provide him what he needs and get what you want in return? For example, if you need to set a limit on your time, is there someone else you can suggest to do the remainder of the work? Of course, you'll probably have to make some trade-offs, but that's why they call it negotiating.

Balancing work and family—
is there such a thing?

A few years back Ellen Galinsky, president and co-founder of the Families and Work Institute, changed the paradigm by suggesting that there is no such thing as "balance." Rather, she thinks what we do each day is navigate between work and family life in a constant series of shifting priorities.[7] Some days you give more to the office, other days it's more about your family's needs.

Call it whatever you want, the seeming tug-of-war between work and family will continue to be a challenge, particularly for women. Though balancing the demands of family and a career is something that men are beginning to grapple with as well, child care is still a responsibility that falls more heavily on women—not to mention housework, elder care, and other related duties.

Years ago work-life balance was considered a soft issue by some executives, secondary to the hard issues that deliver profits. But more and more, people are coming to realize that flexibility is one of the most important issues related to business. If corporations want to attract and retain talent, flexible work arrangements (such as job sharing, working from home, and flexible hours) are necessary. Many companies have these accommodations in place, and some organizational cultures have shifted so that employees are encouraged to take advantage of them. But a lot of institutions still have an unspoken culture that requires face time and very little deviation from the norm. Changing this will take time and a commitment from top-level management that is communicated to all levels of the organization. Creating a new norm needs to be seen as a priority tied to bottom-line profits as well as individual paychecks.

As you progress in your career, you will have trade-offs to consider, and how you deal with them depends on your personal situation—no one way is right for everyone. When my son was young and I had to juggle the responsibilities of work and family, I decided to leave the corporate workplace and start my own business. I thought I would have more control of my hours, which in some ways I did. But when you start a business you have to invest a great deal of time and money. There is no easy solution, but we can learn a lot from women leaders who are handling an enormous amount of responsibility as well as creating their power parameters around family.

I know a woman at an international finance company who was asked to take a top global job. She, her husband, and their two small children resided in the United States, and she didn't want to move or have to travel three-quarters of the time. She knew if she hired the right team, they could do the bulk of the traveling and report back to her. In discussions with top management, this woman expressed her excitement for the assignment and presented her plan to have her team do the majority of travel. That was her power parameter.

To make sure that management understood her commitment to the job, she explained that she would definitely lead the larger, more-critical meetings where strategy was rolled out internationally and her presence would be necessary. In the end, she received the promotion on her terms, and she did an excellent job in her new role. And when her children were older, she actually did take a plum position overseas.

Jill Campbell of Cox Communications is another powerful leader who was able to set boundaries: "I don't work a zillion hours. I can separate the work and the play part of my life. The time that I have with my daughter is most important to me. I have to create those chunks of time. We have a nice breakfast in the morning, I drop my daughter off at school, I'm home at a decent hour, and we have dinner as a family."

Her negotiation is that she has her phone with her 24/7 to stay on top of what's happening. "I feel better if I can check my e-mail to keep connected."

There is no road map for how to manage our family and work commitments. We learn as we go along and accept that things change over time as our needs and the needs of our loved ones change.

Saying yes to yourself

Saying no can give rise to feelings of guilt, but how about trying to see guilt in a new way? As we assert ourselves, the uncomfortable feeling we experience might not be signaling that we're doing something wrong but rather that we're finally doing something right—for ourselves.

Why relegate yourself to the last spot on your to-do list? This problem is so prevalent that I wrote an entire book on the topic called *Time for Me: Simple Pleasures for Women Who Do Too Much.*[8]

Say yes to taking the time for simple pleasures, whatever those may be for you. Start by identifying and getting rid of time bandits, such as guilt, worry, people pleasing, and perfectionism, which I know can be a tall order. But by leaving room in your schedule for the things that nourish and replenish you, you might actually start finding it easier to check off all the other to-dos on your list. For most of us, saying yes to ourselves is an immediate confidence and productivity boost.

Get creative with how you can carve out some me time for yourself. You probably already have in place some things you enjoy. Why not double up on your personal time by doing two at once, like calling a friend when you're exercising. Ask your family in advance which events you can't miss, and make the others negotiable. Be aware of time bandits that eat away at your precious hours. Get a self-care buddy so you can keep each other on track.

These are just a few suggestions. Navigating work life is a complex issue for all of us, and neither side of the equation should be taken lightly.

Confidence spark

In your day planner, make sure to schedule not only your business and family obligations but also your me-time activities. Although you have a certain amount of flexibility, put in pen the personal activities that are nonnegotiable— like doctor visits and a monthly girls' night out. Taking care of yourself will foster your growth on all fronts.

What would you do?

Scenario	Hold yourself back	Create power parameters
Your boss asks, "Can you stay late to finish up a report?" You have already done the bulk of the work, and the report just needs proofing—plus you've stayed late four days in a row.	You agree to finish the report. You want your boss to know that you'll be there no matter what.	You say no. You explain that you need a night to take care of yourself. You suggest your intern, who is eager for more responsibility, pitch in.
Your child asks, "Mommy, please buy me this doll." She has two dolls of the same type on her bed that she doesn't play with.	You buy the doll out of guilt. You've been working late every night for the past week.	You say no. Instead of buying the doll, you find a game you can play with her, and you share some quality time.
Your neighbor says, "Can you bake just one more cake? We don't have enough items for the bake sale." You've already brought her two.	You say okay. The sale is for a good cause, but you resent her for asking you.	You say no. You tell her that you don't have time to bake a third cake. Instead you offer to chip in on buying one.

Power tools

- **Say no.** Saying yes when you are too stretched never yields a good result. You will probably end up resenting the person and yourself.

- **Remember** that saying no can be someone else's yes. Think of turning something down as an opportunity for another person to advance.

- **Be aware** of when you put unrealistic demands on yourself. Treat yourself with kindness and draw the line.

- **Negotiate what you need.** Being clear on what your priorities are and what trade-offs you're willing to make can help you speak up even when you're wary of saying no.

Stand Out and Attract Sponsors

MYTH

The competition for sponsors is fierce—
standing out and getting one is too difficult.

TRUTH

I can attract and build important power alliances.

We all know that being successful in business requires building strong relationships. But do we take enough time to do it? With constant deadlines to adhere to, we may rationalize that sitting at our desks uninterrupted and using the phone and Internet to contact people is enough.

Yes, excelling at our day-to-day tasks is important, and you may be recognized for the excellence of your work, but will that lead to access to higher-ups who can put your name on a slate when a job opens up? Possibly, but don't assume that will happen. Take every opportunity to meet the power players. Get out of your familiar surroundings, and seek out opportunities to mix with those calling the shots.

In the last several years, a lot of buzz has been circulating about sponsors and what they can do to help women advance. In *Smart Women Take Risks* I wrote, "Opportunities happen when someone in charge believes in you and takes a chance on your behalf by opening a door."[1] That someone in charge is a sponsor.

The main difference between mentors and sponsors is that the sponsor relationship is transactional, according to Sylvia Hewlett, author of *Forget a Mentor, Find a Sponsor*. She writes, "A sponsor sees furthering your career as an important investment in his or her *own* career, organization, or vision. Sponsors may advise or steer you, but their chief role is to develop you as a leader. Your role is to earn their investment in you."[2]

Men have had the benefit of others bringing them along more than women have, partly because of our late entry into the workforce. But there is another reason why we may not have attracted these valuable supporters. As women, we are drawn toward people we like; however, the people who can best sponsor us are not necessarily going to be people we like or who are anything like us. As Hewlett explains, what matters in sponsorship is "trust, not affinity."[3]

Michelle Gadsden-Williams, managing director and global head of diversity and inclusion at Credit Suisse, believes that "finding a sponsor whose path or background is different from yours is an excellent learning opportunity. They'll do what's expected—talk you up at meetings when a position becomes available—but they can also give you a different perspective that you might not have had access to otherwise. And you will have something to teach them as well."[4]

We must create strategic alliances with sponsors—whether we like them or not—and show them our loyalty as well as our ability to produce results. These people can catapult our careers. This chapter offers concrete ways for women to cultivate these important alliances.

How to stand out? Deliver!

Produce results by doing your job with energy and enthusiasm. Walk around and get to know people. In meetings, bring your innovative ideas to the table. Take these actions and you will likely get noticed.

The benefits of speaking up and delivering are numerous, and they feed on each other to build your career and your confidence. Producing results increases your chances of getting noticed. What's more, according to 86 percent of the survey respondents who reported feeling confident in the workplace, "using my skills and making an impact" had enhanced their confidence in their own abilities. Then when your achievements are acknowledged and you are singled out for more responsibility, you get another confidence boost. About 70 percent of question respondents said that "acknowledgment from my peers, direct reports, and leaders" also increased their confidence.

As you make your mark, people will likely start paying attention. Several of the women I interviewed attracted sponsors as a result of excellent performance.

"The best relationships come from people who take an interest in you because they see what you are doing and want to help," shared Sandra Dewey of Turner Entertainment and Cartoon Network. She got the attention of Linda Yaccarino when Linda was at Turner (Linda is now president of advertising sales at NBCUniversal). Sandra explained, "She saw my honest efforts to grow and became invested in me."

Another excellent performer was Kim Lubel, now CEO of CST Brands, who took on the general counsel role at Valero Energy when her sponsor, Bill Klesse, moved up to CEO. Around that time, an article was published about how companies that have women in high-level positions are more successful. Kim told me, "I asked Bill if he saw the article, and he looked at me sternly and remarked, 'Do you think I don't know that? Why do you think you're in the role you're in?'"

Being trustworthy, loyal, and dependable are qualities potential sponsors will respect. In addition, accepting assignments that are not on your trajectory show flexibility and a willingness to do what is needed. All of these qualities are what made Jill Campbell stand out at Cox Communications.

Jill caught the eye of Pat Esser, now president of Cox Communications, when she was a general manager and he was in advertising sales. He became a big fan of hers. Like Sandra, Jill credits her ability to produce results as the reason why she stood out among her peers.

"The industry was male dominated and senior leaders saw that I was willing to go where I was needed, and my performance was strong," she told me. "Pat has been one of my sponsors. When he took over the COO role, he had to fill his job and I was promoted to senior vice president of field operations. As he climbed, so did I—he ultimately promoted me to the job I'm in now."

When I got my first "real" job at the *New York Times* as a sales rep, I was so excited about my life. I had a new job, I had just gotten married, and we were living in a dream apartment. I set outrageous goals for myself at work, and my managers were amazed because I reached them. In fact, no one in my department had ever reached the sales goals I achieved. My reputation spread, and I got the attention of the vice president of the division. He would single me out at office functions, make sure he was up to date on my latest accomplishments, and invite me to departmental meetings. I was off to a great start.

After the vice president left, a new group of power players came on board. One of the men took me under his wing.

I was a good listener and ambitious, and I wanted to learn the business. Shortly after, I was promoted. He knew if he needed something done, he could count on me.

Self-promote in a subtle way

An unfortunate workplace truth is that many men self-promote and are respected for doing so, while women sometimes keep quiet about their accomplishments, concerned that they will sound pretentious. However, a big part of standing out and attracting sponsors is letting people know your value.

A senior manager confided that she was turned off by people who were full of themselves and added little value, so she resisted telling people about her achievements. But she realized false modesty doesn't work in business, and that unlike the people with bravado, she brought a lot to the table. Her only regret was that she learned that lesson late in the game.

Subtle self-promotion can be learned. Sure, credit your team if you're a manager, but remember to slip into the conversation that it is *your* team.

Kathy Waller of Coca-Cola has mastered this art. Notice how she describes one of her achievements: "Earlier in my career, *I* convinced senior management to institute new procedures, and *our* team implemented them on deadline." Her skillful use of both "I" and "our" ensured that she as the leader was credited for getting the ball rolling with upper management as well as for her team's on-time implementation.

Michelle Pedigo, senior vice president at MetLife, gave this example: "In a prior job, I received an award as principal of the year. In my acceptance speech, I thanked my team, but it was clear to everyone that it was *my* award."

When I started working at the *New York Times*, I had a male boss who, after shaking hands with a new client, would rattle off one of our team's achievements, making it clear that the team was under *his* direction. I saw him do this time and time again. To teach myself, I would stand in front of the mirror at home and practice. Now I can skillfully slip into a conversation an accomplishment that I am proud of.

 Confidence spark

> Think of one of your accomplishments within the last year. How did you take initiative? What skills did you demonstrate? Who worked with you to make it happen? With this in mind, craft a statement that accurately describes your achievement, using "I" and "we" terms. For example:
>
> - *My* department had 25 percent growth in sales. *(Accomplishment)*
> - *I* researched a new market and suggested *we* pursue it. *(Initiative, demonstrated skills)*
> - Then *the associates* landed the accounts. *(Credit to the people you worked with)*
>
> If you are not used to taking credit, try practicing in front of a mirror like I did. You might also try role-playing with a supportive friend.

It is important not only to speak powerfully but also to put your best foot forward in e-mails and proposals. Tara Mohr in *Playing Big: Find Your Voice, Your Mission, Your Message* suggests not hitting the Send button before checking for unnecessary apologies and undermining disclaimers such as "I'm no expert in this, but . . ."[5]

Developing sponsor relationships

The big question is, how do you attract the attention of a potential sponsor? Start by taking inventory. Who are the power players you know? Do they know what you are capable of achieving? If not, find ways to be more visible. For example, take on a stretch assignment that would catch their attention.

Who are the important people you don't know but would like to meet? Think of whom you know who can set up e-mail introductions. Check LinkedIn for any mutual connections. After you're introduced, ask for an informal meeting.

Do your research—know how your skills can be leveraged to further your potential sponsor's career and vision. When you meet, be clear about what you can offer her and what you would like in return. Remember, sponsoring is a two-way street; the relationship is built on trust and mutual benefit.

Once you have your sponsor's attention, make sure every interaction is well thought out—don't waste her time. That was how Sandra Dewey built her relationship with Linda Yaccarino. She was judicious about asking Linda for time, and when she did, she used that time wisely to get practical advice. "I came prepared and I wasn't pushy, demanding something she didn't want to offer me," Sandra explained.

At Valero Energy, Kim Lubel would think up three things she wanted to talk about with her sponsor, then CEO Bill Klesse, when they were both in town. "I'd try to find time to sit with him in the mornings and hear what was on his mind. I'd come with a little sticky note of three things I'd wanted to get across. We'd sit and talk through them."

Both Sandra and Kim came prepared. Because your interactions with your sponsor are time sensitive, picking your issues is important. Not everything is of equal importance.

A relationship with a sponsor can strengthen and evolve over time. When I was calling on companies for the funding of a television show, I got through to a high-level leader of a major Fortune 500 company. I researched her career path before the call, and I had a friendly conversation with her lovely assistant, who made sure our appointment was scheduled. This leader and I spoke for twenty minutes over the phone, and I was very passionate—the program I was pitching was about women advancing in the workplace. I heard a few weeks later that she was on board.

I introduced her to senior people who were advocates for diversity and kept her abreast of the latest developments and research. She in turn had me host several events at corporate headquarters. I helped create her company's first women's employee resource group. She introduced me to the CEO, and I interacted with him on several occasions. She also invited me to several external functions attended by the company's senior women leaders.

Although many of our interactions were over the phone or through e-mail, face time was important. Every few months, either she came to New York or I was at her headquarters involved in an event.

Like the other sponsor relationships I've talked about, ours was mutually beneficial and manifested a sense of loyalty and trust. That trust was built over years of working together, similar to the sponsor relationship of Kathy Waller and Gary Fayard, the former CFO of Coca-Cola.

"We've worked together for many years, and he absolutely knew if he needed something from me, he would get it," Kathy told me. She delivered for Gary, and he in turn made sure she was considered for top jobs—including the CFO role when he retired.

Sylvia Hewlett describes sponsorships as a "long-range quid pro quo."[6] Be prepared to make a time investment in these relationships. Believe me, you'll find it pays off in spades. According to research from the Center for Talent Innovation, sponsored women are more satisfied with their rate of advancement than their unsponsored peers.[7]

See yourself as your sponsor sees you

Sometimes a sponsor's vision of where you fit in an organization is different from what you see for yourself. If your sponsor sees you taking on more responsibility, but you are unsure of your abilities, trust her estimation of you. She is putting herself on the line for a reason.

When Lisa Quiroz recruited Jackie Hernández to take over as publisher of *People en Español*, Jackie felt somewhat shaky about stepping up. She told me, "I was filling some really big shoes. I thought, *Oh my God, this is a huge job; can I handle it?*" But she trusted Lisa's assessment of her, coupled with the confidence her parents had instilled in her. And, of course, she took the job. She was right to do so because the magazine thrived under her leadership.

You may not understand why a job is the right fit, but if your sponsor is suggesting it, give it a try. Kathy Murphy of Fidelity Personal Investing did exactly that when she was at ING. Tom McInerney, former CEO, was her sponsor, and he challenged her to take an assignment that initially was not of much interest to her. She had been deputy general counsel, and he asked her to be the chief compliance officer. "My response was, 'Are you kidding me?'" she related. "But taking that job was a turning point—it got me closer to the business."

If your sponsor thinks you are ready to move to a higher level, then you are. Even if you feel a little nervous, take the next step, as Kim Lubel of CST Brands did—more than once. Coming from a small town in Ohio, Kim's role models were nurses, teachers, or stay-at-home moms. She herself came from a long line of teachers; her grandmother, mom, and older sister worked in the classroom. Kim assumed that she would follow in their footsteps.

"In college I majored in Spanish and international studies, so I planned to either teach, go to grad school, or get a job in government," she shared. One of her professors, who helped her get a scholarship to earn a master's degree, thought that she would be successful in a different career. "Later on he encouraged me to pursue a law degree, something I had never thought of doing," Kim said. "He saw something in me I hadn't seen in myself." Sure enough, Kim was an asset to the legal profession.

Then in the summer of 2009 when Kim was general counsel at Valero Energy, her sponsor, CEO Bill Klesse, sent her to an executive management program at Stanford Business School. The classes showed her that she had an intuitive sense of how to manage.

"When I came back from that program, Bill asked me if I could be CEO one day and I responded yes. Before I went to Stanford, I probably would have said no," Kim told me. By having a high-powered executive support her growth and help her to acknowledge her strengths, Kim realized that she could tackle bigger challenges, and she did.

As you move up in the organization, paying it forward is important. Acknowledge those that are starting out who are delivering results. Take time to extend yourself and figure out a way they can increase value for the company and support your visions. Be available as a sponsor, and encourage other leaders to do the same.

What would you do?

Challenge	Hold yourself back	Succeed with sponsors
You are assigned to a project with a leader whom you've identified as a potential sponsor.	You keep a low profile as you do the work. You don't want to look like you're showing off or sucking up.	You are instrumental to the project's success, and you make it your business to touch base with the leader on several occasions.
You are at a company event and see a power player you would like to meet.	You want to approach him, but too many people are vying for his attention. You don't get your chance.	You've done your homework and know where he is taking the company. You've thought about how you can help him get it there. Even though a group of people is surrounding him, you don't leave until you make initial contact.
Your sponsor says she's going to suggest you for a high level job.	You are hesitant because you don't think you're ready for that level of responsibility.	You say yes because you trust her judgment. You assess your strengths relative to the job and ask her for feedback for dealing with areas where you don't have experience.

Power tools

- **Deliver good work** consistently, and let others know what you are doing. Word spreads quickly, and you may get on the radar of a potential sponsor.

- **Ask yourself** what you can uniquely contribute to your organization. Identify a few senior people who can help you accomplish this objective, and be clear on ways you can advance their agenda and yours.

- **Identify someone** as a potential sponsor, and then seek out a way to interact with her informally. Slip into the conversation your desire to support her initiatives.

- **Build relationships** with more than one person as a good career investment. Strong alliances grow and change. People retire or take on assignments that can make it difficult to stay in touch.

Trust Your Inner Compass

MYTH

When I am under pressure, I can't tap into my intuitive insight.

TRUTH

I always have access to my intuition and the ability to use it.

Here is what successful people have had to say about trusting your inner compass:

Oprah Winfrey: "Follow your instincts. That's where true wisdom manifests itself."

Albert Einstein: "The intuitive mind is a sacred gift and the rational mind is a faithful servant. We have created a society that honors the servant and has forgotten the gift."

Gisele Bündchen: "The more you trust your intuition, the more empowered you become, the stronger you become, and the happier you become."

Steve Jobs: "Don't let the noise of others' opinions drown out your inner voice. And most important, have the courage to follow your heart and intuition."

How do leaders reach their positions of power? How did they know when to take the smart risks that led to their success? What fueled their decision-making processes? Often, you will hear them say that in the end, they relied on their intuition.

Research shows a positive correlation between intuition and business success. In a 1976 article in the *Harvard Business Review*, management guru Henry Mintzberg notes that the use of intuition "may be more important at the top of an organization."[1] Perhaps higher-level managers have less time to make decisions and more leadership experience to draw on.

You may have already noticed my many references to intuition throughout the book. I believe that listening to your inner voice is key to making the right decisions for your career. Tara Mohr talks about the "inner mentor"—"an imagined version of an older, wiser you" that you can access for guidance.[2] With discipline and practice, we can learn to connect with our intuition more, no matter our age or position. And as we begin to follow the direction of our inner compass, we will feel more ready to take the smart risks necessary to advance professionally.

Make intuition your business edge

I've gone over the many ways that gender biases make the workplace a more challenging environment for women. At times we can find ourselves being swayed by prejudices that we know aren't true. And when that happens, we may doubt our abilities. Intuition, a faculty that I believe women are underutilizing, can get us back on track.

Although intuition is often thought of as a feminine trait, research from Hayes, Allinson, and Armstrong, as well as others, shows that women are not necessarily using their intuition more than men at work.[3] Hayes and Allinson also found that using intuition has more to do with job level and position than gender.[4] Women may also be trying to avoid being judged by the female stereotypes of being "too emotional" or "irrational."

When we ignore our inner voice, we are shortchanging ourselves. Your inner voice is a compass always giving you signals about which way to turn—it is your unique professional edge. Careful and judicious use of this kind of emotional intelligence is a plus, helping us make the right decisions and boosting our confidence in our choices. In the Women and Confidence Survey, we asked respondents: "What would your adult self say to your younger self to inspire her to have more confidence?" The answers underscored the importance of listening to your intuition with responses like, "You are smart. Trust your gut instincts!"

Take this example: As a baby boomer, I really prize the opinions of millennials when it comes to social media. They grew up using these tools, so I usually trust their judgment. When a young woman whom I respect advised against a new form of graphic posts I was considering for our business Facebook page, I began to question the merit of my idea. At the same time, my gut sense was to give it a shot anyway. I'm glad I listened to my inner voice because those graphic posts were a huge success. My years of experience and my wide knowledge of our audience fed into my instinctive decision, leading me to make the right choice, and now we reach millions of people around the world who are inspired by our page.

Most of the women leaders I interviewed told me that they listened to their inner compass when making important decisions. Sandra Dewey of Turner Entertainment and Cartoon Network, shared that she believes intuition helps us to become effective, confident decision makers.

Debbie Storey of AT&T has her own take on intuition. She uses her intuitive ability to make business decisions, but explained that intuition is not some unrefined, magical gut instinct. Rather, it stems from a rapid processing of data points that come from years of experience.

This view of intuition is backed up by journalist and noted author Malcolm Gladwell. In *Blink: The Power of Thinking without Thinking*, he argues that what people perceive as intuition is simply rapid cognition.[5] He explained in a Q and A on his website that rapid cognition is "thinking that moves a little faster and operates a little more mysteriously than the kind of deliberate, conscious decision-making that we usually associate with 'thinking.'"[6] Gladwell writes that in the first two seconds of appraising a situation, you bring to bear all of your beliefs, attitudes, values, and knowledge of similar past experiences. He calls this process "thin-slicing," which is "the ability of our unconscious to find patterns in situations and behavior based on very narrow slices of experience."[7]

A gut feeling is a compilation of all your knowledge distilled into a simple impulse. Your intuitive sense stems from the rapid processing of everything you already know, everything you have learned and experienced. We can trust in our vast stores of life experiences to help us take the next professional leap.

Even those in the most analytical positions can benefit from intuition, as Charisse Lillie of Comcast shared. "I'm a lawyer, so I'm trained to be logical. You collect the facts, analyze the data, and come up with a few solutions. From this you try to figure out which one is going to get you to your goal, wreaking the least amount of havoc. But intuition is at play for me too—following my gut."

Charisse gave an example of how she followed her intuition at a previous job. She had to develop a book of business for the law firm. Her mentor questioned the value of her bar association work and encouraged her to focus only on getting her name out to general counsels who could give her business. However, her gut told her to stay with it. She followed her instincts and eventually served as chair of the American Bar Association's Commission on Diversity, something she was very passionate about. Ultimately, this position was an important platform that helped her develop a great deal of business.

I believe that intuition is a higher form of knowledge. When we get still enough to connect with it, we know which actions are the right ones to take. Several of the survey respondents agreed that a connection to something greater helps them make the best decisions. One woman wrote, "Believing in a power greater than myself keeps me grounded, focused, and invigorated, thus allowing me to be the best I can be."

However you define it—gut instinct, intuition, inner compass, or inner voice—when we veer away from it, we are vulnerable to making bad choices. As Jacqueline Hernández of Telemundo put it, "Intuition is core to who we are. When we question it, we start to question the truth."

Using your intuition to make better choices is a process. It consists of considering your options and listening to your inner guidance to choose the right one. As we begin to trust our intuition and see how it helps us make better business decisions, we will find that relying on our instincts for all sorts of choices will get easier.

⤡⤢ Confidence spark

Reflect back on times when you trusted your gut sense, and it was right. Also bring to mind times when you knew you should have but did not. What transpired as a result? Now take a fresh look at a challenge you are facing. What is your intuitive sense of how to handle it? Create an action plan based on that.

Consider your options using intuition

When our inner compasses tell us that we are making the right decisions, our ability to step up and move forward is boosted. We may still be shaky about what will happen next, but knowing we can trust our instincts and ourselves is the foundation for taking action.

For any decision we have to make, we have at least four options: moving straight ahead, proceeding with caution, waiting to act, or deciding that it's not right for us. The following examples demonstrate how the women I interviewed used their intuition to consider their options and make some tough decisions.

Move straight ahead

When presented with an opportunity, you may know that you should proceed, whether others agree or not. In the story below, Jackie Hernández felt strongly about how Telemundo should be rebranded, and she was able to get the market research to support her choice. She moved straight ahead without hesitation.

"We decided to relaunch the brand, and for two years we did a tremendous amount of research. We used to have a beautiful blue *T*—the logo was very traditional. My gut told me to go with red because it's a vibrant color, and we deal with Hispanic culture. We also wanted something that was contemporary and modern. We asked consumers what they thought. I got enough information to back up my gut reaction and went with it. The relaunch was a huge success."

Proceed with caution

Some opportunities create doubt, but not enough to stop you from moving forward. Although Jill Campbell of Cox Communications considers herself a high risk taker, she proceeds with caution when necessary. She looks both ways and then takes a leap in the direction of her inner compass. Below is the story of when she took a lower-titled position in order to move ahead. "I actually went backwards for one of my jobs. I was managing a cable system and they asked me to fill the number two spot in a larger one, so I lost the status of being a general manager. But it was the best move I could have made because I was able to learn how to run a big system. That set me up to be the general manager of other big systems. It was a gut feel on that one."

Wait, then decide

Sometimes sitting on a decision for a while to gather all the information—including what is *not* being said—and connecting with what your intuition is telling you is important. Such was the case with Susan.

Susan had been with her company for two years as a senior director, and she was one of two people being considered for a promotion to vice president when her boss retired. In conversations with him, the implication was that she was next in line. Around the same time the decision was being made, a recruiter called about an amazing opportunity as president of a pharmaceutical division. Her skills were in demand!

Susan wasn't sure about the new opportunity for a number of reasons. First, she had a good chance of being made vice president at her current company. Second, this new job would be a big jump in levels. She waited an entire week before she accepted the interview for the president position. In the end, she trusted her instincts about who was shooting straight and who had other agendas: "I thought about it a lot. I kept coming back to the fact that I didn't trust my boss—I knew he didn't want to lose me (he did not want to have to train someone else), but I don't think he wanted to promote me either. That's what my gut told me. After several rounds of interviews, I was offered the job, which I accepted—best move I ever made."

↘↙↗↖ Confidence spark

Think of the person who is your strongest supporter—did you sense at the beginning that you could trust him? Now think of someone you know professionally, a person you keep your distance from. Did you know not to trust him initially? Don't discount your first reaction to people; it is usually right.

Decide it's not right

If your inner voice is advising no, then it's an indication that an opportunity is not right for you. Even if the opportunity is presented as being in your best interest, have the courage to turn it down if that is what needs to happen. For Kathy Murphy of Fidelity Personal Investing, saying no is a matter of being able to sleep at night because she made the right decision. In the world of financial products, competition is intense, but she has learned to follow her inner compass and only offer products that have a positive value proposition for the consumer.

"My rule is that if we are not comfortable selling it to our own parents, then we shouldn't sell it to anyone. I would take the hit with our sales figures because I didn't want the reputational risk. It's a much better way to grow the business long term . . . and you can sleep at night!"

What would you do?

Scenario	Hold yourself back	Trust your inner compass
Your boss is discussing a potential problem, and team members are weighing in. You are privy to some information and have a gut sense that action should be taken now.	Your inner compass is drowned out by the assertive voices in the room, and you retreat. You don't want to seem pushy.	The issue is important, and you assert that action needs to be taken and say why. You offer next steps.
Your client contact has been promoted, and she introduces you to her replacement. You sense he is insecure and only looking out for himself.	You ignore your gut feeling and tell him about a minor problem with the account. Later you hear through the grapevine that he's complained about how you handled things.	You limit your interaction with him by delivering what is needed and nothing more. You realize that the best way to deal with someone you don't trust is to communicate only what is necessary.
You've been offered a position with a start-up division. Your intuition is advising you to accept, even though doing so involves some risks.	You decide to play it safe. A start-up is risky. You're not sure you're ready for that.	You ask a trusted advisor's opinion, and she sees the long-term possibility of advancement, which confirms what you sense. You decide to go for it.

Power tools

- **Don't shortchange yourself**. Your intuition is your unique professional edge. Rely on it more.

- **Practice trusting your intuition** for all sorts of choices. Your first reaction to people and the difficult situations that are presented to you is usually right.

- **Let your inner compass decide** which course to take in making a decision: move straight ahead; proceed with caution; wait, then decide; or decide it's not right.

Conclusion

At this very moment, you have everything you need to take a leap—your strengths, talents, intuition, imperfections—all of your different parts. Trust your impulse to make a difference—to speak up and introduce an idea or to go for a bigger position.

Keep moving forward even though mad mind-chatter may be telling you to hold back. Don't accept that negative self-talk as truth. Question it. The truth is that you are talented beyond measure, and the time for personal change is now. The world needs every bit of your resourcefulness.

These last pages will help prepare you to step up in a new way. Let the inspiring words of these risk-taking leaders support you. They took action even when they felt shaky, and each of them is better off for it. I encourage you to do the same.

"Trust that you are ready."
Debbie Storey, Chief Diversity Officer of AT&T

If you're asked to do a stretch assignment, go for it even if you don't feel ready. If your supervisor thinks you can do it, trust her judgment.

There were times in my career where I was given a job and I felt sick to my stomach. I thought, *I do not have any knowledge that will allow me to succeed in this job.* On one occasion, there were forty people around the table, the smartest people in the business, who had been managing the operation for thirty years. I kept thinking, *I'm sitting at the head of the table and I have to solve this problem.* What helped me get through it was that I told myself, "My managers would not have put me here if they did not think I could do it."

I went home that night and realized I was brought here because of my set of skills. I told myself, "Go back to those skills that you know you do well, and do it here."

"Mentally promote yourself."
Kathy Waller, Chief Financial Officer of Coca-Cola

Changing the way you behave can be difficult as you advance. Give yourself permission to show up as a leader with power and presence.

When you get a promotion and you find yourself at a different level in the organization, you have to respond, act, and react differently in line with the new expectations. You have to mentally promote yourself to that next level.

"Ride the wave."
Jackie Hernández, Chief Operating Officer of Telemundo

When you're in charge of a demanding project, you can pull back out of fear or you can grow into your new responsibilities and learn from the experience.

My dad told me to face my fears and dive in. Toward the end of his life, he became very ill, and we would talk about work.

One time he brought up the beach to make his point. He said, "You have to ride the wave or else it'll knock you over." That was a great piece of advice.

"Be open, but know your guardrails."
Kathy Murphy, President of Fidelity Personal Investing

You have to be willing to try new things. You also have to know where you stand and what you will not accept.

Be open to new assignments—it's the only way to grow. But you need guardrails—you need to know the things you want to do and things for which you have absolutely no interest or passion.

In a previous company, I was asked to consider leading technology and operations, but it would have separated me from serving our customers, which is my passion. I knew I could add much more value in a job that was more closely tied to getting results for them. I quickly declined that job and have never looked back!

"Give feedback; it is a gift."
Jill Campbell, Chief Operations Officer of Cox Communications

Giving feedback is a way of paying it forward. Feedback can mean the difference between a person's advancement or derailment.

Even if it's not something the other person wants to hear, you're doing it because you want the individual to develop. You are not giving it from a point of meanness, but a place of respect.

"Pick your battles wisely."

Charisse Lillie, Vice President of Community Investment of Comcast Corporation and President of the Comcast Foundation

Every battle does not have to be fought. Every argument is not worth winning.

> You have to figure out which ones are important enough for you to take a stand. Take those two or three and really stick with them. Have a plan and then execute on that plan.

"Know your audience."

Sandra Dewey, Executive Vice President and Head of Business Affairs, Turner Entertainment Networks and Cartoon Network Originals

In order to get your ideas across you need to know where other people are coming from.

> You have to get into the mind of your bosses or your junior people—whether you're talking to a group or having an intimate conversation. The more you practice this, the more effective you're going to be.

"Let your passion lead you."

Kim Lubel, Chief Executive Officer of CST Brands

Being excited about what you do is what differentiates a dynamic career from an unfulfilling one.

> Don't look for opportunities just to move up a ladder. You want to be passionate about what you do. I tell my daughters this all the time, "You need to love what you do; if you don't, you're not going to be successful. It's just going to be a job." We spend too many hours at work for it not to be a passion.

"Keep good company."

Helene Lerner

It's important to have women in your life who support and honor your growth. Many of you may already have this, but if not, I encourage you to reach out to new people and mobilize that support for yourself. Gather a few women to discuss the ideas you've read in this book and do some of our exercises. You want to encourage each other to think bigger and take some smart risks. You'll find a lot of tools on my website (http://www.WomenWorking.com). And use our social media pages for contacts and inspiration (WomenWorking.com on Facebook, @WomenWorking on Twitter, and the WomenWorking group on LinkedIn).

Power tools

- **Fear can be your ally.**
  Take the initiative to speak up, even if you are shaky. What you're advocating for is more important than your fear. Come from a position of service. Act as if you can do it and you will be able to. Remember our new take on confidence: acknowledging fear and moving forward anyway.

- **Leadership presence is attainable.**
  Pay attention to what women at higher levels say and do—adapt their styles to what works for you. Dress the part, be self-aware, understand your audience, artfully listen, and maintain composure.

- **The truth will catapult your growth.**
  Feedback helps you advance. Use your intuition to discriminate between what is useful and what is not. Ask for feedback if you're not getting it.

- **Saying no can be a good thing.**
  Create power parameters to keep you focused on important tasks. Protect your time, set boundaries, and make your no someone else's yes.

- **Alliances with power players are mutually beneficial.**
  Take every opportunity to make yourself visible to the power players around you. Be strategic and see how your skills and expertise can be useful to a higher-up you want to work with. Build a relationship with a sponsor based on mutual benefit and trust.

- **Intuition is your edge.**
  When you follow your inner compass, you feel more confident taking the smart risks necessary to advance professionally. Listen to your inner voice and use it to help you make better business decisions that benefit you, the people you serve, and your company.

Appendix A

Thirty Days of Confidence Sparks

This bonus section contains thirty Confidence Sparks to help you strengthen your ability to move forward even when shaky. Some are reflections; some are calls to action. Read one each morning for the next thirty days. You don't need to go in order, and you can repeat a Confidence Spark. Pick the one that seems most appropriate for any given day. Sit in a comfortable chair where you will not be disturbed, and if you feel like it, write down your insights in your journal.

- Think of a challenging situation in which you would really like to speak up but haven't yet. Imagine how you would act. What would you say? Role-play with a friend if needed, and set a time to address the issue with the appropriate person.

- Don't pay attention to those who don't have your best interests at heart. If a disparaging comment comes your way today, keep focused on your goals.

- Zero in on your priorities. Even though you have a lot do, do you find yourself gravitating to the low-impact items on your to-do list? What are you avoiding and why?

- Choose a women leader you admire. What qualities does she possess? Of those, which do you already have and which do you need to develop? Get suggestions from an advisor on how to chart a course of action.

- Think of a higher-up in your corporation who would be a good contact for you. How can you meet him? Do you know someone who can introduce you? Do your homework before you meet. How can you help advance one of his goals?

- Picture your professional life in a bigger way. Think of the position you eventually want to have and the skills that will be required. Write down the skills you already possess and the ones you need to strengthen. Talk to an advisor about your goal—what does she think you need to work on?

- Don't let self-doubt get the best of you. If you are in a position of power and responsibility, know that you have what it takes to be there. Others believe in you— prove them right.

- Think of a challenging person in your life and jot down things about him that you know are definitely true. Recognize the assumptions you might be projecting onto him. Do new insights come to mind?

- Own your strengths as well as your weaknesses. Reflect on how you can turn one of your weaknesses into a strength. Ask a coach or mentor for suggestions on how you can improve. Start doing the work to make this happen—one small action at a time.

- Leave some room in your day to recharge. Make sure you take a lunch break. When you treat yourself right, you are better able to accomplish the work-related priorities on your list.

- The unease you feel when you step out in a new way is natural—discomfort equals growth. Try something beyond the scope of what you've done, whether that means making a pitch in a meeting or approaching a higher-up at a business function.

- Take stock of all you do. Jot down the highlights of your accomplishments in a given week. Slip one of your achievements into a conversation with a supervisor. Remember, humble pie doesn't work in business.

- Are you having a difficult time assessing some feedback that you've received? Run the matter by a trusted advisor who knows you. Work with her to take what fits and discard the rest.

- What do you need to deal with that you've been ignoring? To address your fear, examine the worst-case scenario if you were to take action. That scenario probably won't happen, so commit to taking one action toward handling the situation.

- Think of someone you have just met. What motivates him? What is his agenda? Try practicing artful listening to find out. Listen to what he says, but also observe his gestures and tone of voice. What is your intuition saying about him and where he stands? You'll know whether or not to make him an ally.

- Are you putting an unrealistic demand on yourself? Adjust your expectations, whether that means changing your timetable or recruiting others to help. Be kind to yourself.

- Give up guilt. Guilt only serves to keep you stuck. You will never be able to please everyone, so don't second-guess yourself about your choices.

- What do you think should be your next big step? Advancing is impossible without taking some calculated risks. Even if your decision turns out not to be the best choice, you will learn some valuable lessons that will help you.

- Do you get defensive when you receive unexpected negative feedback? Be aware of what you are feeling and what you are telling yourself when it happens. Try to pause rather than react. Processing it later on, when you have some distance from the comment, is better.

- What do you see as your strengths? Choose one and reflect on how you can leverage it to step out in a bigger way. Make a list of actions to take and a timetable of when you will take them.

- Are you withholding feedback from a peer or mentee that would be valuable to him or her? If so, why? Know that you and the person will both be better off if you speak up.

- Nothing will ever go exactly as planned. Your friend will be running late, your colleague will misunderstand your instructions—whatever it is, let it go and move on.

- You have a whole lifetime of experiences and insights. Trust your gut reaction when you're faced with a challenging situation. Ask for input when you need it, and then take decisive action.

- Did you recently say yes to a request that you didn't really want to do? How did you feel afterward? Can you go back to the requester and say no, and suggest someone else or another way of handling the situation?

- How can you stay calm when the stress of a project mounts? What can you tell yourself that would lessen your anxiety? Write down your answers while you're feeling clearheaded. Keep them in mind the next time you start feeling stressed.

- Reflect on a time when you negotiated successfully. Why do you think you were successful? What techniques did you use to make your goals something that the other person also wanted? Use these insights to help with your next negotiation.

- Strive to do your best, but let go of perfectionism. Think of a task that has been consuming your time. Know that what you've already done is good enough. Next!

- What steps can you take to build a stronger bond with a higher-up, like sending her an article of interest or connecting her with a useful contact? Commit to doing at least one of these things this week.

- Does your body language project confidence? Are you slouching or standing straight? Do you make eye contact or do you avoid it? If you felt more confident, what would that look like? Act as if you feel self-assured whether you do or not.

- Give yourself the credit you deserve. In what ways have you grown in the last six months, and how have you been able to change the lives of other people?

Appendix B

The Women and Confidence Survey: Methodology and Results

In my work, I am constantly asked how women can develop more confidence. Confidence is a hot topic on forums, at conferences, and in informal discussions among career women. This book mostly reflects my own advice and understandings, developed through years of work and thought on the question of confidence. However, knowing that I wanted to write a book on it, I decided to harness the good thinking and experience of other professional women.

Survey background

To capture data systematically, we established the Women and Confidence Survey, asking working women about confidence both at work and at home. We tapped our robust WomenWorking.com network, asking women to weigh in. We also publicized a link to the survey on social media outlets. With one of the groups on LinkedIn, Citi's Connect: Professional Women's Network, I asked, "What does confidence mean to you? What enhances and inhibits it?" and gave the link to the survey. Our post was one of the group's top discussions at the time. Clearly, I had struck a nerve.

In consultation with researcher Susan Adams at Bentley University, we also sent the survey to some of the university's students and alumni. Bentley was an ideal research partner for this venture due to its strong graduate and undergraduate emphasis on business, and its focus on women's leadership, spearheaded by Bentley president Gloria Larson and Betsy Myers, founding director of the Center for Women and Business.

Survey methodology

The survey comprised twenty-one multiple-choice, open-ended, and demographic questions (reproduced below with basic answer statistics). We conducted the survey from April through June of 2013 by sending the link to the survey to our WomenWorking.com network, several LinkedIn professional groups, and our own social media channels (Facebook, Twitter, and LinkedIn) to capture data from those most interested in women's leadership and confidence. To ensure age diversity among respondents, we also sent the survey link to a select group of Bentley students and some alumni.

We deliberately chose not to try to recruit a nationally representative group of respondents. Instead, the sample represents data from a group of business-minded and professional people, mostly women, many of whom are at the managerial level. This group finds confidence to be a major issue on a daily basis. The women in this sample were, on the whole, more confident than women in the general population, were generally older, and had achieved greater success. The goal, therefore, is not to represent women as a whole but to help all women learn from the wisdom, experiences, and lessons learned from this generally high-confidence group.

The survey recruitment was successful, and a total of 535 responses were received. Results were generally examined using a chi-squared test. A large enough sample was required to establish statistical differences at the 90 percent confidence level.

Survey instrument

The results for each question in the survey are presented below.

1. How do you define confidence?

520 responses (free-writing)

2. Where do you think confidence comes from?

Answer	Response percentages
You're born with it	<1.0%
You develop it over time	37.0%
A combination of both	55.8%
Other	5.4%
No responses	<1.0%

3. **Which of the following sources have contributed to your confidence?** (Check all that apply.)

Answer	Response percentages
Acknowledgment from my family, friends, peers, and superiors	73.9%
A wealth of experience—educational, professional, and personal	85.0%
A connection with my "higher self" that transcends challenging times	55.5%
Other	17.2%

4. **Which of the following behaviors have served to build your confidence?** (Check all that apply.)

Answer	Response percentages
Acknowledging my strengths and how they serve others	83.9%
Becoming more aware of negative self-talk and challenging it	61.4%
Recalling past experiences when I've acted courageously	56.3%
Other	17.9%

5. **Confidence is connected to:** (Check all that apply.)

Answer	Response percentages
Being motivated about your life	73.3%
Feeling in sync with other people	39.8%
Having the courage to try new things	79.8%
The ability to demonstrate your strengths	78.8%
Other	13.7%

6. **Does confidence look different for men and women?**

Answer	Response percentages
Yes	50.4%
No	27.1%
I don't know	21.1%
No responses	1.3%

7. **Do you feel confident in your workplace?**

Answer	Response percentages
Yes	84.4%
No	14.5%
No responses	<1.0%

8. **If you feel confident in your workplace, which of the following practices have enhanced your confidence?** (Check all that apply.)

Answer	Response percentages
Having a leader or mentor who appreciates and respects me	66.3%
Meeting my deadlines and staying on top of my work	67.3%
Being recognized formally with promotions and raises	44.0%
Acknowledgment from my peers, direct reports, and leaders	70.3%
Using my skills and making an impact	86.3%
Other	12.4%

9. **If you don't feel confident in your workplace, which of the following practices have inhibited your confidence?** (Check all that apply.)

Answer	Response percentages
Having a leader who micromanages and disrespects me	53.5%
Missing deadlines and falling behind	20.5%
Having colleagues who are uncooperative and overly critical	45.7%
Feeling disconnected to my job because the work does not leverage my skills	49.2%
Other	20.2%

10. **Do you feel confident in your personal life?**

Answer	Response percentages
Yes	83.7%
No	15.3%
No responses	<1.0%

11. **If you do feel confident in your personal life, which of the following practices have enhanced your confidence?** (Check all that apply.)

Answer	Response percentages
I surround myself with people who believe in me	60.2%
I was led to believe early on that I could achieve anything I worked for	52.5%
I have a sense of myself that is not dependent upon what others think of me	67.7%
I feel I can impact my surroundings	66.6%
I feel I can make mistakes and recover from them	76.4%
Other	11.7%

12. **If you don't feel confident in your personal life, which of the following practices have inhibited your confidence?** (Check all that apply.)

Answer	Response percentages
My friends and family don't take me seriously	17.5%
I can't measure up to the expectations of others	24.8%
I can't measure up to my personal expectations	54.9%
I don't feel I have much impact	29.1%
Fear of failure	48.0%
Other	16.3%

13. **Is there a difference between how confident you feel at work or at home?**

Answer	Response percentages
Yes	57.5%
No	41.6%
No responses	<1.0%

14. **What would you do if you had more confidence?**

Answer	Response percentages
I would say no to things without feeling guilty	42.1%
I would say what I think, regardless of the opinions of others	35.4%
I would end unhealthy relationships	29.5%
I would reach for higher career and personal goals	57.8%
Other	15.5%

15. **Do you have a belief in a power greater than yourself? If so, how does that affect your confidence?**

403 responses (free-writing)

16. **How does your level of confidence affect the risks you are willing to take?**

511 responses (free-writing)

17. What might you do to become more confident?
(Check all that apply.)

Answer	Response percentages
Take a course on the topic	16.7%
Do more inner reflection	48.5%
Read a self-help book	26.8%
Counter negative mind-talk with more affirming thoughts	58.2%
Find a "confidence buddy" to hold you accountable for taking self-affirming actions	32.9%
Seek out a coach or a therapist	34.8%
Other	20.7%

18. What would your "adult self" say to your "younger self" to inspire her/him to have more confidence?

514 responses (free-writing)

19. What age range do you fall into?

Answer	Response percentages
20 or under	<1.0%
21–25	6.7%
26–30	9.5%
31–35	11.7%
36–40	9.9%
41–45	13.4%
46–50	16.4%
51+	30.4%
No responses	<1.0%

20. What best describes your current position?

Answer	Response percentages
Unemployed	3.9%
Student	2.6%
Freelancer	3.3%
Entry-level employee	5.0%
Experienced nonmanager	24.4%
Mid-level manager	18.5%
Senior manager	15.3%
Business owner	7.2%
Entrepreneur	7.2%
Stay-at-home mother	<1.0%
Educator	2.4%
Retired	<1.0%
Other	7.8%
No responses	<1.0%

21. What gender do you identify with?

Answer	Response percentages
Female	95.1%
Male	2.9%
Other	1.1%
No responses	<1.0%

Notes

Introduction

1. Katty Kay and Claire Shipman, *The Confidence Code: The Science and Art of Self-Assurance—What Women Should Know* (New York: Harper Business, 2014), 17–18.
2. See appendix B for full survey background, methodology, and instrument.

Chapter 1

1. "Make Innovation Fun," WomenWorking.com, March 2013, http://www.womenworking.com/how-make-innovation-fun.
2. Sheryl Sandberg, *Lean In: Women, Work, and the Will to Lead* (New York: Knopf, 2013), 8.
3. Georges Desvaux, Sandrine Devillard-Hoellinger, and Mary C. Meaney, "A Business Case for Women," *McKinsey Quarterly* (2008): 4.
4. "Make It Happen: Mentors, Dreams, Success," first potential broadcast September 1, 2002, presented by South Carolina Educational Television, distributed by American Public Television, a production of Creative Expansions Inc.
5. "In Her Heels," WomenWorking.com, July 2011, http://www.womenworking.com/her-heels.
6. "Make a Real Impact," WomenWorking.com, January 2012, http://www.womenworking.com/make-real-impact.

Chapter 2

1. Sylvia Ann Hewlett, *Executive Presence: The Missing Link between Merit and Success* (New York: Harper Business, 2014), 24.
2. Ibid., 145.
3. "Is It Arrogance, No!" WomenWorking.com, September 24, 2014, http://www.womenworking.com/it-arrogance-no.

4. Hewlett, *Executive Presence*, 65.
5. Ibid., 98.

Chapter 3

1. Sheryl Sandberg, *Lean In for Graduates* (New York: Knopf, 2014), 105.

Chapter 4

1. "How to Be Happy in 2014," *World One*, CNN International, first broadcast, January 20, 2014.
2. Jessica Valenti, "She Who Dies with the Most 'Likes' Wins?" *The Nation*, November 29, 2012, http://www.thenation.com /blog/171520/she-who-dies-most-likes-wins#.
3. Sandberg, *Lean In for Graduates*, 65.
4. Hannah Riley Bowles, Linda Babcock, and Lei Lai, "Social Incentives for Gender Differences in the Propensity to Initiate Negotiations: Sometimes It Does Hurt to Ask," *Organizational Behavior and Human Decision Processes* 103, no. 1 (2007): 84–103, doi: 10.1016/j.obhdp.2006.09.001.
5. Sandberg, *Lean In for Graduates*, 60.
6. Ibid., 59.
7. Ellen Galinsky, "Moving beyond Perfectionism and Finding a Work-Life Fit: Lessons from Marissa Mayer and Anne-Marie Slaughter," *Huffington Post*, July 20, 2012, http://www .huffingtonpost.com/ellen-galinsky/marissa-mayer_b_1690577 .html.
8. Helene Lerner, *Time for Me: Simple Pleasures for Women Who Do Too Much* (Illinois: Simple Truths-Sourcebooks, 2015).

Chapter 5

1. Helene Lerner, *Smart Women Take Risks: Six Steps for Conquering Your Fears and Making the Leap to Success* (New York: McGraw-Hill, 2006), 61.
2. Sylvia Ann Hewlett, *Forget a Mentor, Find a Sponsor: The New Way to Fast-Track Your Career* (Massachusetts: Harvard Business Review Press, 2013), 20.
3. Ibid., 21.

4. "Building Relationships with Sponsors," *WomenWorking.com*, October 2013, http://www.womenworking.com/building -and-maintaining-relationships-sponsors.

5. Tara Mohr, *Playing Big: Find Your Voice, Your Mission, Your Message* (New York: Gotham Books, 2014), 197–198.

6. Hewlett, *Forget a Mentor*, 20.

7. Sylvia Ann Hewlett, Kerrie Peraino, Laura Sherbin, and Karen Sumberg, "The Sponsor Effect: Breaking through the Last Glass Ceiling," *Harvard Business Review* (December 2010): 10, http://www.globalwomen.org.nz/site/globalwomen/files/pdfs/The%20 Sponsor%20Effect.pdf.

Chapter 6

1. Henry Mintzberg, "Planning on the Left Side and Managing on the Right," *Harvard Business Review* 54, no. 4 (1976): 57.

2. Mohr, *Playing Big*, 63.

3. John Hayes, Christopher W. Allinson, and Steven J. Armstrong, "Intuition, Women Managers and Gendered Stereotypes," *Personnel Review* 33, no. 4 (2004): 403–417.

4. Christopher W. Allinson and John Hayes, "The Cognitive Style Index: A Measure of Intuition—Analysis for Organizational Research," *Journal of Management Studies* 33, no. 1 (1996): 119–135; and Christopher W. Allinson and John Hayes, *The Cognitive Style Index: Technical Manual and User Guide* (Harlow, UK: Pearson Education, 2012), available online at http://www .talentlens.co.uk/assets/legacy-documents/71874/csi-manual .pdf.

5. Malcolm Gladwell, *Blink: The Power of Thinking without Thinking* (New York: Penguin Books, 2006) 23.

6. "Blink Q and A with Malcolm," gladwell.com, http://gladwell .com/blink/blink-q-and-a-with-malcolm/.

7. Gladwell, *Blink*, 23.

Acknowledgments

I want to offer special thanks to the following people: Kim Lubel, chief executive officer of CST Brands; Jill Campbell, chief operations officer of Cox Communications; Sandra Dewey, executive vice president and head of business affairs, Turner Entertainment Networks and Cartoon Network Originals; Jacqueline Hernández, chief operating officer of Telemundo; Charisse Lillie, vice president of community investment of Comcast Corporation and president of the Comcast Foundation; Kathy Murphy, president of Fidelity Personal Investing; Debbie Storey, chief diversity officer of AT&T; Kathy Waller, chief financial officer of Coca-Cola; and the other amazing women leaders who contributed to this book.

I want to thank Neal Maillet and Jeevan Sivasubramaniam, whose enthusiasm about this project was welcome support. Thanks also to my interns Andreia Bulhao, Jessica Benmen, and Amanda Miller who made our work seem easy. Jessica, you went way beyond the call of duty and it is appreciated. Thank you to Susan Adams of Bentley University for distributing our Women and Confidence Survey to some of their students and alumni and reviewing the data, Andrew Acosta for the interpretation of the data, and to my good friend Laura Newberry for her abounding encouragement. I want to thank Joel Fortinos and Becky Post for their guidance, as well as Danielle Lucie Goodman and Shauna Lani Shames for their insights and craftsmanship. I am grateful to the Turkey Land Cove Foundation for providing a magical place to write this book.

In some examples, the women mentioned in this book are not actual people but composites representing the experiences of several colleagues, clients, friends, or acquaintances. On occasion names have been left out to provide anonymity.

Index

mentors/mentorship (*continued*)
being your own mentor, 17
*Forget a Mentor, Find a
Sponsor* (Hewlett), 71
importance of, 3
inner mentoring, 83
Mintzberg, Henry, 83
mistakes, perfectionism and,
21
Mohr, Tara, 75, 83
moving straight ahead (using
intuition), 87–88
Mulcahy, Anne, 18
Murphy, Kathy
candor as respect, 50–51
declining opportunities, 95
giving feedback, 46
reading the room, 30–31
saying no, 90
sponsor relationships, 78
myths and truths
confident women, 5
feedback, 42
intuition/inner compass, 82
leadership presence, 25
not having needed skills, 17
power parameters, 55
preparation for career
stages, 12
sponsorship, 70
transferring fear, 9

negative attitude, 4–5, 11, 12
negative beliefs, 14–15
negative feedback, 50

negotiations
for balancing life and work,
65
making trade-offs, 63, 69
power parameters, 61–63
win-win rule of, 63
nervous energy, 16–17

opinions, 18
opportunities
declining, 90, 95
looking for, 96
uncertainty about, 88–89
overachievement, 16

passion, 96
paying it forward, 79, 95
people-pleasing behavior, 11,
56, 57, 104
people sensitivity, 41
perfectionism
being realistic about, 59
letting go of, 21–22
and sting of feedback, 44
picking your battles, 26, 96
*Playing Big: Find Your Voice,
Your Mission, Your Message*
(Mohr), 75
poise under pressure, 26–28,
28–29
positive attitude, 20
power of your fears, 11
power parameters
balancing work and family,
64–66

Yaccarino, Linda, 72, 76

Zintz, Andrea, 27, 45–46
Zuckerberg, Mark, 57

About the Author

Helene Lerner is the founder of WomenWorking.com. She is a prolific author, independent public television host, Emmy-award-winning executive producer, and workplace consultant. She covers a wide array of issues, such as women and confidence, harnessing personal power in changing times, calculated risk taking, reinvention, breaking barriers, and more.

Since 1994 Helene has produced and hosted more than twenty televised specials under the umbrella of her company, Creative Expansions, Inc. She received American Public Television's MVP Award for her outstanding contributions to public television. She began her career as a teacher in the New York City public school system. Using her innate business instincts, Helene later pursued sales and marketing assignments during the 1980s, working her way up through the management ranks of the *New York Times*. She is currently the CEO of Creative Expansions, Inc., a multimedia company she created whose mission is to empower women and girls.

In addition to writing books and producing television specials, Helene maintains a private practice, coaching individuals and groups and providing tools to increase their sense of empowerment. She also advises corporations on leadership and diversity issues. A member of Phi Beta Kappa, Helene holds an MBA from Pace University and a master's in education from City College in New York City, where she currently resides.

Her website, WomenWorking.com, the premier website for career women, offers strategies on leadership, advancement, and navigating work and life, as well as a multimedia blog with posts from career coaches. She has a robust social media presence, providing tips and inspiration to loyal followers.

Facebook: Womenworking.com
Twitter: @Womenworking
LinkedIn: WomenWorking group

Berrett–Koehler
Publishers

Berrett-Koehler is an independent publisher dedicated to an ambitious mission: *connecting people and ideas to create a world that works for all.*

We believe that to truly create a better world, action is needed at all levels—individual, organizational, and societal. At the individual level, our publications help people align their lives with their values and with their aspirations for a better world. At the organizational level, our publications promote progressive leadership and management practices, socially responsible approaches to business, and humane and effective organizations. At the societal level, our publications advance social and economic justice, shared prosperity, sustainability, and new solutions to national and global issues.

A major theme of our publications is "Opening Up New Space." Berrett-Koehler titles challenge conventional thinking, introduce new ideas, and foster positive change. Their common quest is changing the underlying beliefs, mindsets, institutions, and structures that keep generating the same cycles of problems, no matter who our leaders are or what improvement programs we adopt.

We strive to practice what we preach—to operate our publishing company in line with the ideas in our books. At the core of our approach is stewardship, which we define as a deep sense of responsibility to administer the company for the benefit of all of our "stakeholder" groups: authors, customers, employees, investors, service providers, and the communities and environment around us.

We are grateful to the thousands of readers, authors, and other friends of the company who consider themselves to be part of the "BK Community." We hope that you, too, will join us in our mission.

A BK Business Book

This book is part of our BK Business series. BK Business titles pioneer new and progressive leadership and management practices in all types of public, private, and nonprofit organizations. They promote socially responsible approaches to business, innovative organizational change methods, and more humane and effective organizations.

Berrett–Koehler
Publishers

Connecting people and ideas
to create a world that works for all

Dear Reader,

Thank you for picking up this book and joining our worldwide community of Berrett-Koehler readers. We share ideas that bring positive change into people's lives, organizations, and society.

To welcome you, we'd like to offer you a free e-book. You can pick from among twelve of our bestselling books by entering the promotional code **BKP92E** here: http://www.bkconnection.com/welcome.

When you claim your free e-book, we'll also send you a copy of our e-newsletter, the *BK Communiqué*. Although you're free to unsubscribe, there are many benefits to sticking around. In every issue of our newsletter you'll find

- A free e-book
- Tips from famous authors
- Discounts on spotlight titles
- Hilarious insider publishing news
- A chance to win a prize for answering a riddle

Best of all, our readers tell us, "Your newsletter is the only one I actually read." So claim your gift today, and please stay in touch!

Sincerely,

Charlotte Ashlock
Steward of the BK Website

Questions? Comments? Contact me at bkcommunity@bkpub.com.

MIX
Paper from
responsible sources
FSC
www.fsc.org **FSC® C002589**

Certified

Corporation
bcorporation.net

31901056205133